The Books of the Bible

Zondervan Quick-Reference Library

ZONDERVAN
QUICK
REFERENCE
LIBRARY

The Books of the Bible

John H. Sailhamer

ZondervanPublishingHouse

Grand Rapids, Michigan

A Division of HarperCollinsPublishers

The Books of the Bible
Copyright © 1998 by John H. Sailhamer

Requests for information should be addressed to:

📖 ZondervanPublishingHouse
Grand Rapids, Michigan 49530

Library of Congress Cataloging-in-Publication Data

Sailhamer, John.
    The books of the Bible / John H. Sailhamer.
        p. cm. — (Zondervan quick-reference library)
    ISBN: 0-310-50031-1 (softcover)
    1. Bible—Introductions. I. Title. II. Series.
BS475.2.S244 1998
220-dc 21
                                 97-39133
                                     CIP

Interior design by Sue Vandenberg Koppenol

Printed in the United States of America

98 99 00 01 02 03 04 /❖ DC/ 10 9 8 7 6 5 4 3 2 1

Contents

Abbreviations
of the Books of the Bible

Genesis	Gen.	Matthew	Matt.
Exodus	Ex.	Mark	Mark
Leviticus	Lev.	Luke	Luke
Numers	Num.	John	John
Deuteronomy	Deut.	Acts	Acts
Joshua	Josh.	Romans	Rom.
Judges	Judg.	1 Corinthians	1 Cor.
Ruth	Ruth	2 Corinthians	2 Cor.
1 Samuel	1 Sam.	Galatians	Gal.
2 Samuel	2 Sam.	Ephesians	Eph.
1 Kings	1 Kings	Philippians	Phil.
2 Kings	2 Kings	Colossians	Col.
1 Chronicles	1 Chron.	1 Thessalonians	1 Thess.
2 Chronicles	2 Chron.	2 Thessalonians	2 Thess.
Ezra	Ezra	1 Timothy	1 Tim.
Nehemiah	Neh.	2 Timothy	2 Tim.
Esther	Est.	Titus	Titus
Job	Job	Philemon	Philem.
Psalms	Ps(s).	Hebrews	Heb.
Proverbs	Prov.	James	James
Ecclesiastes	Eccl.	1 Peter	1 Peter
Song of Songs	Song	2 Peter	2 Peter
Isaiah	Isa.	1 John	1 John
Jeremiah	Jer.	2 John	2 John
Lamentations	Lam.	3 John	3 John
Ezekiel	Ezek.	Jude	Jude
Daniel	Dan.	Revelation	Rev.
Hosea	Hos.		
Joel	Joel		
Amos	Amos		
Obadiah	Obad.		
Jonah	Jonah		
Micah	Mic.		
Nahum	Nah.		
Habakkuk	Hab.		
Zephaniah	Zeph.		
Haggai	Hag.		
Zechariah	Zech.		
Malachi	Mal.		

Introduction

What Is This Book?

The *Zondervan Quick-Reference Library: The Books of the Bible* is a new and unique reference tool. Simply put, it is a complete and succinct commentary on each book of the Bible that you can read in approximately one minute, only a fraction of the time it takes to use a traditional commentary. The commentary goes right to the point—the exposition of the book itself. You get a simple, clear statement of the content of each book of the Bible. This book not only takes into account the latest in biblical scholarship, it also shows the sense and place each book occupies within the larger structure of the Bible.

Because we get so much of our information in daily life quickly and efficiently, we are becoming increasingly accustomed to having information or knowledge about the Bible given to us in the same way. Though the need for fast delivery systems often undercuts the role of thoughtful reflection in our society, our habits have changed. There is therefore a legitimate need for a more efficient way to build our knowledge of the Bible—if only as a starting point for more in-depth and reflective understanding. It is a truism in learning that once we get a sense of what a book is about, the details of that book make more sense.

A regular use of this book should lead to a more in-depth and knowledgeable study of God's Word. It can, of course, be used along with traditional commentaries and Bible study tools, and this book is not intended to replace them. Rather, our aim is to supply the legitimate need (or appetite) for efficiency in obtaining Bible knowledge. It is a convenient starting point.

This book has three distinct features: (1) a series of brief introductory pages, intended to bring the reader up to speed on the study of the Bible; (2) a commentary on each book of the Bible, listed in the order they occur in the English Bible; (3) a glossary of important terms and themes used throughout the commentary. The reader should pay close attention to the third feature. Whenever you encounter unfamiliar terms or themes, look them up in the glossary. The glossary can also be read to gain an understanding of general biblical themes.

What Is the Bible?

The Bible is one book made up of many books. These were written over many centuries by authors with vastly different backgrounds and cultures. Many authors are well known: Moses, David, Solomon, Ezra, Paul. Such men are not only the leading characters in the Bible, they are also its leading producers. A surprisingly large number of the biblical authors, however, are nameless. Who wrote 1 and 2 Kings, for example, or the book of Hebrews?

Fortunately, the answer to questions of this nature is of no major consequence in understanding the Bible. Who doesn't know and appreciate an old Hollywood movie from the 30s and 40s? Yet how many know about Irving Thalberg of MGM or Jack Warner of Warner Brothers Studios? These were the men who made or produced the movies; they were the "authors" of those films. But we know the movies by watching them, not by learning about their authors and producers. Similarly, we know the Bible and the books of the Bible by reading them.

Some kinds of books (e.g., a diary) require some information about its author before it can be properly understood. Other books, like works of literature and history, are written so that you don't have to know the author to understand and appreciate them. What you need to know is given to you as you read the text. The Bible is that way: It is written simply to be read.

This may sound obvious, but many biblical scholars disagree. The Bible is often approached today as a book so different from other books and so distant from our world that we need to learn all about its world before we can understand what it says. Though there is some merit to that process, it ignores the fact that the Bible was written with a general audience in mind. Their authors were sensitive to the limitations of time and culture that future readers might encounter. They thus took these limitations into consideration when they wrote their books.

If there was a particular historical or cultural item they felt needed explanation, they did so (see 1 Sam. 9:9). What they didn't feel needed explaining was general knowledge (like what the moon is) or unimportant items (like the color of Sarah's eyes). For the most part, they allow the readers to fill in the blanks of their stories. We, of course, often fall back on popular conceptualizations. But whether Moses looks like Charlton Heston in DeMille's *The Ten Commandments* or Michelangelo's Moses does not affect our understanding of Exodus.

The Bible Is the Word of God

Although the Bible shares features with many other kinds of books, it is a unique book. It is the Word of God. We should say something here about what this statement means. Basically it means two things: (1) The Bible is divine revelation, and (2) the Bible is divinely inspired.

The Bible teaches that God has left signs of his existence and power in his work of creation. From the world around us and from within our own selves we can see evidences of God's glory. For example, from the world around us we see that he is a powerful and wonderful God; from within our own consciences, that he is a personal and holy God. But there is a limit to what can be known about God in that way. Apart from the Bible, for example, we cannot know God's will or God's love for us. We may know from within ourselves that we need God's grace and mercy, but without God's personal speaking to us we cannot know how to receive it. In the Bible God has made known his will for us.

But how does God speak to us in the Bible? It does so like any other book—with letters, words, sentences, and paragraphs. The Bible is a written text. If we can read, we can read the Bible. This all sounds elementary, but it is important. Sometimes the idea is cast about that the Bible is nothing more than human thoughts and aspirations about God. The Christian idea of revelation is much more than that. The Bible may be human words, but those words express the very words that God wants us to know.

How can human words express God's will? The answer to that question leads to the notion of *inspiration*. The books of the Bible were written by human beings who were "carried along" in their writing by the Holy Spirit (2 Peter 1:21), but the Bible never gets more specific than that. It does not tell us *how* the Holy Spirit moved these writers to express God's will. We can safely say that God did not dictate the words of the Bible to the writers, nor did he merely give them suggestions on what to write. In the clear statement of Scripture, its written words are "God-breathed" (2 Tim. 3:16). What the human writers wrote, God intended to say to us.

The Canon of Scripture

It is one thing to talk about the Bible in general terms, but just exactly what Bible are we talking about? Isn't there some disagreement on what books are even in the Bible? The answer, of course, is that there is disagreement, but not as much as one might think. The standard for what books are in the Bible and what books are not is called the *canon*.

For the Old Testament, the standard was determined long before the birth of Jesus. We have little direct knowledge of the process that brought this about, but we can say with certainty that the Old Testament we have today is the same Scriptures that Jesus used. It was the accepted standard of the Jews in the first century.

In some parts of the church, in the early centuries A.D., additional books were put alongside the canon of the Old Testament in some manuscripts of the Bible. These were popular works that were used in worship and devotion. Later on some of these works were accepted as part of the canon by the Roman Catholic Church and some Orthodox Churches, though not having the same authority as the Bible. These books (up to eighteen) are called the Apocrypha.

There is no dispute about the canon of the New Testament. At an early stage in the history of the church, the New Testament canon was closed, and no new books were added.

The basis for including a book in the canon of the Old and New Testament was twofold: (1) universal acceptance among God's people—Israel for the Old Testament and the church for the New Testament; (2) internal witness of the Holy Spirit—the Spirit of God bore witness to the early readers of Scripture that these books and no others were the inspired Word of God.

How do we know the early church accepted the right books and genuinely witnessed the Spirit's confirmation? For the Old Testament we have the confirmation of Jesus. Throughout his ministry, Jesus quoted and used the Scriptures as God's Word. To accept his authority is to accept the authority of the Old Testament. For the New Testament we have the confirmation of the apostles—the authoritative men who had received direct instruction from Jesus during his earthly ministry. Their acceptance and confirmation of the canon of the New Testament assures us of its authority in our lives today. In this way the authority of both the Old Testament and the New Testament is grounded in the authority of Christ.

What Is the Old Testament?

The Old Testament is also the Bible of Judaism, where it is called simply the "Hebrew Bible." To speak of an "Old" Testament acknowledges the existence of a "New" Testament. Unfortunately, calling it the "Old" Testament also may imply it has been superseded by the New Testament. That is not the case. The New Testament itself and the Christian church acknowledge the full authority of the Old Testament for the Christian life. By means of these Scriptures, Paul says, the Christian "may be thoroughly equipped for every good work" (2 Tim. 3:17).

Christianity shares the Old Testament with Judaism because Jesus was a Jew and because he saw the whole of his life as a fulfillment of the ancient Jewish prophets' hope in the coming Messiah. Christians believe Jesus is the Messiah long expected by the Old Testament prophets. The Old Testament is thus the basis of the New Testament. Without it the New Testament has little meaning. When John the Baptist, for example, saw Jesus, he said, "Look, the Lamb of God, who takes away the sin of the world" (John 1:29). Without the Old Testament notion of the sacrificial Passover lamb (Ex. 12:23) and the prophet Isaiah's messianic Servant of the Lord who was to give his life as a ransom for sin (Isa. 53:6), John's words cannot be understood.

Long before the birth of Jesus, Jews reverenced and searched their Hebrew Scriptures. They had a deep and sincere hope regarding God's faithfulness to his Word. God, for example, had promised David that a royal son would be born to his house who would rule in peace over Israel and all the nations (1 Sam. 7). Those who wrote the Old Testament had as one of their primary goals the preservation of that hope for generations to come.

Those who collected and preserved the various books of the Old Testament and grouped them into their present form were also motivated by an intense expectation of the coming Savior. The scribe Ezra had much to do with that process (e.g., Ezra 7:10). During his time, the greatest part of the work of collecting and shaping the books of the Old Testament occurred.

An ideal picture of the faithful Jew awaiting the fulfillment of the Old Testament promises can be seen in the old man Simeon, who waited at the temple "for the consolation of Israel" and who immediately recognized Jesus as the promised Savior (Luke 2:25–32).

The Unity of the Old Testament

The basic structure of the Old Testament canon is different in the Hebrew text than in our English Bibles. In the latter the historical books are placed together, as are the poetic books, the prophetic books, and so on. But in the Hebrew Bible, the books are arranged according to their content and central themes, with the following threefold order:

(1) The Law (Pentateuch). Genesis, Exodus, Leviticus, Numbers, Deuteronomy
(2) The Prophets. Former: Joshua, Judges, Samuel, Kings
    Latter: Isaiah, Jeremiah, Ezekiel, Twelve Minor Prophets
(3) The Writings. Psalms, Job, Proverbs, Ruth, Songs of Songs, Ecclesiastes, Lamentations, Esther, Daniel, Ezra, Nehemiah, Chronicles

The chief difference between this and the English Bible lies in the location of the prophetic books, the poetic books, and the later historical books (Ezra, Nehemiah, and Chronicles). Also, Daniel is not included among the prophetic books and Ruth is not in with the historical books.

Some biblical books have later additions attached to them that cannot be traced back to the original authors. The death of Moses, for example, is attached to the end of the Pentateuch (Deut. 34:5–10)—surely not added by Moses himself. An exhortation to watch for the return of Elijah was added to the end of Malachi (Mal. 4:4–6). These two additions include similar material. The end of Deuteronomy alludes the coming of a prophet "like Moses . . . who did . . . miraculous signs and wonders." Similarly, the end of Malachi speaks of the return of the prophet Elijah, who, we know from the historical books, did great signs and wonders like Moses. Elijah was a prophet like Moses, and Elijah was coming again!

These two additions are strategically located at the seams of the large sections of the Old Testament canon. Significantly, they also correspond to the additions placed at the beginning of the books of Joshua and Psalms. Joshua begins with an exhortation to meditate day and night on the Law of Moses; he who does so will prosper (Josh. 1:8). This is the same exhortation offered in Psalms1:2–3, even using the same words!

Shaping of the Hebrew Canon

Pentateuch	Former Prophets	Latter Prophets	Writings
	Joshua–2 Kings		
Deut. 34:9–12	Josh. 1:1–9	Mal. 3:22–24	Ps 1.

Such convergence of material suggests a deliberate shaping of the Old Testament canon. The Old Testament has been made into a single, unified book.

The Shaping of the Old Testament

The Old Testament received its present shape sometime after the return from Babylon (539 B.C.)—a crucial period in Israel's history. It was a time of severe testing for God's people, for their hope and faith in his promises had all but been dashed to pieces. It seemed as though those promises had not only not come about, but were less likely than ever to be fulfilled. Daniel, for example, waiting for the fulfillment of God's promises to the fathers and pouring over the prophetic books, wonders out loud why the prophetic words have not yet been fulfilled (Dan. 9:1–2). In reading Jeremiah, he understood Jeremiah to say that the Messiah and his kingdom would come at the close of the seventy years of the Captivity (see Jer. 25:11). But the Captivity had ended, and there was still no Messiah. Daniel cannot understand what went wrong.

God answered Daniel's prayer by sending the angel Gabriel to reveal the precise time of the coming of the Messiah. Gabriel told Daniel that the Messiah would not come at the conclusion the seventy years of Babylonian Captivity. Why not? Because, as Daniel's prayer of confession shows (Dan. 9:4–19), Israel had not remained faithful to God's covenant and thus was not ready for the Messiah. His coming would be delayed until their transgression was complete and their wickedness atoned (9:24), which would not happen until after sixty-nine "weeks" of years (9:25–26)—that is, after some 483 years. The traditional reckoning of years from Daniel's day to the coming of Jesus fits comfortably within that time frame.

In other words, the Old Testament Scriptures were collected and shaped during the darkest hour of Israel's history. The people needed renewed hope in the promises of God. Those who gathered and formed the various books of the Old Testament into the single collection we now possess were eagerly awaiting the coming of the Messiah. They read the Scriptures with that hope in mind, and their expectation is reflected in their work. At the same time, that expectation was a result of the themes inherent in the books they were shaping. Thus, the shape they gave to the final form of the Old Testament was a reading sequence that enabled its readers to see more clearly the picture of the Messiah.

What Is the New Testament?

The New Testament is the authoritative collection of God-breathed writings. Its books were written by the disciples of Jesus, the apostles, and its main teaching is that the Old Testament promise of the "new covenant [or testament]" (Jer. 31:31) was fulfilled in the death and resurrection of Jesus (Luke 22:20; 2 Cor. 3:6).

The New Testament is shaped around a fourfold purpose. (1) Its initial purpose is to present, in narrative form, the birth, life, death, and resurrection of Jesus Christ. The four "Gospels" each describe events in the life of Jesus. They cite specific messianic prophecies that show how Jesus' life and death fulfilled Old Testament promises.

(2) The rejection of Jesus by the people of Israel, the Jews of his own day, meant that the kingdom promised in the Old Testament would not be established exactly as foretold. But what did happen? What is the church's relationship to the Old Testament promises of the kingdom? To answer these questions the book of Acts was written. Acts explains how a fundamentally Jewish remnant of believers in Jerusalem became, in a short time, a primarily Gentile church, spread throughout the ancient world.

(3) The letters of Paul and the other apostles are devoted to the establishment and development of the Gentile churches. These letters were intended to establish guidelines and basic norms for all churches. They become increasingly concerned about doctrine and the problem of false teachers.

(4) The New Testament concludes by focusing on the return of Christ to establish his kingdom on earth (Revelation).

We learn something about the books of the New Testament by noting how they are arranged. The Gospels provide the basis of all the teaching that follows. Matthew, the most comprehensive, comes first, followed by Mark, a kind of summary. John is inserted between Luke and its sequel, Acts, perhaps because of John's emphasis on the Holy Spirit. In Acts 28 Paul is in Rome, preaching the gospel. This book is then followed by his letter to the Roman church, and then by the rest of his letters. Then comes Hebrews, which explains the deeper matters of the gospel. The general letters and Revelation close the New Testament.

The Old Testament

Genesis

The book of Genesis is the introduction to the Torah and the rest of the Bible. It introduces and develops the central characters and themes of the Bible story. The main characters are God, humankind, and the chosen people, Israel; the main themes are human failure, divine grace, and hope.

The narrative begins with God's creation of the world, including his special creation of human beings and his preparation of the land that he wished to give to his people, Israel (Gen. 1). This was a good land, and those whom he created to dwell in and enjoy this land were put there to worship and obey him (ch. 2). Foolishly, the first man and his wife turned away from God, their Creator, and sought to find another way to life and prosperity (ch. 3). That way ended in divine judgment and death: the first couple was expelled from the garden God had made for them (ch. 3); their first child was a murderer (ch. 4); the first civilization was destroyed by a flood (chs. 6–9); and the first great city, Babylon, humankind's only hope apart from God, was abandoned in ruins (ch. 11).

In the midst of that divine judgment, however, came the promise of grace and redemption. God's promise of a redeemer who would crush the head of the serpent (Gen. 3:15) strikes an early note of hope. This hope reverberates throughout the subsequent chapters of Genesis and finds its full exposition in the last words of Jacob: a mighty conqueror would arise from the house of Judah and establish God's rule over all the nations (49:8–12). The lineage of that promised redeemer is traced from Eve to the family of Noah (ch. 5), to Shem (ch. 10), to Abraham (chs. 11–25), to Isaac (ch. 26), and to Jacob (chs. 27–50), finding its ultimate fulfillment in that mighty king from the house of Judah.

When the nations were dispersed from the city of Babylon (Gen. 11), God chose Abraham and brought him back to the land prepared in creation and gave it to him and his descendants. From among those descendants, God promised to provide blessing for all humanity. Abraham would become a great nation, God would bless that nation, and through it all the nations of the earth would be blessed (12:2–3).

The Genesis narratives go to great lengths to show that God alone would ultimately fulfill his promise. God's people continually fell short of his call. Looking to their own strength, like Adam and Eve they often sought to find a way apart from God. However, God was patient. He continually watched over their weaknesses and provided the right help at just the right time. Isaac was born in his mother's old age when there was no longer hope for a son. Jacob obtained his older brother's birthright and blessing by God's grace—even before his birth and in spite of his many later attempts to rob and steal them from his brother. Through God's providential care, during a time of severe famine, Judah and his brothers were brought safely to Egypt—in spite of their attempts to kill their brother and savior, Joseph.

Exodus

The book of Exodus opens four hundred years after the close of Genesis (cf. Gen. 15:13), with the people of Israel, heirs of God's promise of redemption, suffering under cruel oppression in Egypt (Ex. 1). Their anguished cries, however, did not go unheeded. The Lord remembered his promise to their ancestors and raised up a deliverer, Moses, to bring them back to the land he had prepared for them (chs. 2–4). In keeping with God's plan, Israel's deliverance became an occasion to make himself known to the nations. God thus displayed his power before the Egyptians through ten "signs" performed through his servant Moses (chs. 5–11). Their rivers were turned to blood, their land was infested with swarms and pestilence—not to afflict divine wrath on this nation, but to reveal God's glory (7:5). This was the same God who desired the salvation and blessing of all the nations (Gen. 12:3). The sacrifice of the Passover lamb, with its blood applied to the doorpost (Ex. 12–13), and the Israelites' baptism in the Red Sea (chs. 14–15; cf. 1 Cor. 10:2) pointed to how God would one day accomplish that salvation in Christ.

God had further plans for his people. He wanted to restore to them the fellowship he desired with all human beings, created in his image. He thus entered into a covenant with Israel at Mount Sinai (Ex. 16–19). That covenant called for obedience to God's will and personal holiness. God desired that his people come to him as persons, willing to have personal fellowship with him. Thus all forms of idolatry were strictly forbidden. Instructions, sometimes extending to minute detail, were given so that there be no misunderstanding what God's will was (chs. 20–24). Most of all, the covenant entailed the worship of the one and only true God.

Though the Israelites agreed to follow God's will and obey the covenant, they quickly forsook the Lord and made for themselves an idol, a golden calf (Ex. 32). This meant a total departure from the kind of relationship God had intended for them. The covenant thus came to an abrupt halt. Moses shattered the stone tablets of the covenant, and the people were severely punished. Only the grace of God (34:6–7) ensured a renewed covenant and continued fellowship between God and his people.

Because of Israel's disobedience, God gave them even more laws and became more specific in the kinds of obedience he required. But God continued to live among his people, even instructing them in detail on the kind of "house" he was to have among them. That house, or tent, was called the tabernacle. This structure they built in the desert, following the plan God laid out (chs. 25–40). Since the plan was a copy of God's dwelling in heaven, the tabernacle served to bring heaven to earth. Such a condescension on God's part to live among an unholy people necessitated stringent measures to protect his holiness (see Leviticus).

Leviticus

The book of Leviticus continues the line of thought at the end of Exodus. Now that the tabernacle had been constructed and completed, its use had to be explained. To give the reader some idea of the nature of the covenant relationship between God and Israel, the author describes the required procedures for the sacrifices and offerings (Lev. 1–7), the duties of the priests (chs. 8–16), and the need for holiness on the part of everyone (chs. 17–27). From the way these texts were written, it is obvious that they were not intended for the priests to use as their own instructions. They were rather intended to show the general reader the various duties of the priests and the nature of Israel's religion.

Central to the rituals and holy actions is the concept of atonement. A holy and righteous God cannot overlook wickedness or lawlessness. Building on the lessons of the earlier narratives in the Torah, the book of Leviticus assumes that the only just penalty for a blatant act of disobedience to God's will is death (cf. Gen. 2:17). It also takes for granted that human beings have gone astray from God's way and have sought their own means of finding blessing. The fall of Adam and Eve in the Garden of Eden foreshadowed the fall of the people of Israel in the incident of the golden calf (Ex. 32).

But God is a gracious God (Ex. 34:6). In spite of Israel's repeated failures, he continued to renew their covenant. He himself provided a means of substitution whereby the death rightly due sinful human beings was transferred to an innocent animal. God accepted the blood shed by the innocent animal as a substitute for the blood of the guilty sinner. Throughout Leviticus, that system of sacrifice is assumed as God's gracious gift to atone for sin.

Though this book never mentions it, there was a latent inequity in its system of sacrifices. Already in the Old Testament that inequity was felt. David, for example, says in the Psalms, "O Lord . . . you do not delight in sacrifice, or I would bring it; you do not take pleasure in burnt offerings" (Ps. 51:15–16). This same theme is picked up in the New Testament: "It is impossible for the blood of bulls and goats to take away sins" (Heb. 10:4). These sacrifices thus served more as a reminder of sin and the need for atonement than as an actual removal of guilt. They had to be repeated regularly to cover the guilt of the people. Thus something more was necessary to make atonement permanent. That something more, as the New Testament teaches, comes "through the sacrifice of the body of Jesus Christ once for all" (Heb. 10:10).

Numbers

Optimism, mixed with dread and foreboding, fills the book of Numbers. The optimism can be seen in the elaborate plans made for the triumphant journey of the people out of the desert and into the Promised Land (Num. 1–10). The people were ready. They were organized into family groups. The tabernacle had been built, and the Lord was about to lead them into Canaan. Though wonderful, these events were almost too good to be true. Given the failures of these people in the past (e.g., Ex. 32) and the failures of the whole of the human race that preceded them (e.g., Gen. 3), how can we, the readers, expect them to succeed in this covenant?

A tinge of dread and foreboding already makes itself felt early on in the narrative. Along with the reminder of the ongoing need for purity of life were warnings against treachery and jealousy (Num. 5). Then, out of nowhere, came a complaint from the people (11:1a). They had forgotten their anguish in Egypt and saw only their hardships in the desert. The alert reader can be heard saying, "Here we go again." Sure enough, God's anger was rightly aroused at their complaints, and a fire from heaven came down on them (11:1b).

Though the fire receded after Moses's prayer, we soon learn that this was only a prelude to further complaints and rebellion (Num. 12–14). In the end the people prove faithless (14:11–12), following the discouragement of the ten spies who said the land could not be taken. They were thus denied the blessing of enjoying the Promised Land. Instead, they had to wander for forty years in the desert and ultimately die there. As so many times before, God continued to care for their needs, but this time they had forfeited their blessing. They would not enter the Promised Land. That would be left to the next generation under the leadership of Joshua (see the book of Joshua). As was the case in the earlier books, the narrative that recounts the rebellion of the people is followed by the imposition of additional laws (chs. 15–19).

The second half of the book picks up with the new generation of Israelites after forty years in the desert. Moses himself proved faithless and thus could not accompany the new generation into the land (Num. 20:12). What a striking message to the reader! Moses, the servant of God, who was the preeminent example of obedience to God's laws, could not inherit the Promised Land because he failed to believe God. The lesson here is that the law does not lead to faith in God. The law is good, but it will not produce faith.

But God continued with his people, making their way to the edge of the Promised Land. Try as they would (chs. 21–25), the nations could not halt the Israelites (chs. 26–35). Those whom God has blessed, no one can curse; God turns the curses of their enemies into blessings.

Deuteronomy

As this book opens, Moses is standing on the edge of the Promised Land, unable himself to enter, delivering his farewell address to the people. His purpose is to explain the meaning of God's law (Deut. 1:5). The name "Deuteronomy" means "second law," and its use as a title stems from the fact that much of this book repeats the earlier laws Moses had given the people.

Moses begins by reviewing God's care and concern for his people during their years in the desert (Deut. 1–3). For the most part this review summarizes what happened to them ever since they departed from Sinai. At the close of this survey, Moses turns to the new generation of Israelites, about to enter the Promised Land, and calls them to be obedient to God's law (ch. 4).

Moses' purpose is to draw out the central message of the Sinai narratives (Ex. 19–33). He begins by laying again the foundation of the Ten Commandments (Deut. 5). From these ten statements, Moses draws the inference that central to Israel's relationship with God is the need for fear and love (ch. 6). On the surface these two ideas seem to be at cross-purposes. How can one fear God and love him at the same time? But for Moses these two ideas fall together under the larger heading of obedience. Fear (that is, reverence and awe before God) can lead to obedience of God's will in the same way that love can.

The main body of the book summarizes the many instructions God had given Israel for living in the Promised Land (Deut. 12–26). These instructions focus on all aspects of the people's lives: worship (chs. 12–16), leadership (chs. 16–18), and the affairs of everyday life (chs. 19–26). Stern punishments are prescribed for those who fail (chs. 27–28). For this new generation to live according to these instructions requires a virtual new covenant, based on a new heart (chs. 29–30). Moses, who is not optimistic that Israel will prove any more faithful to this covenant than their parents were at Sinai (31:27–29), nevertheless looks far into the future, to a time when God will give his people a new heart (30:6a). Then they will love God (30:6b), keep his commandments (30:8), and walk in his ways (30:14). The missing factor, then, is a new heart.

As a source of hope and encouragement for the people until they receive that heart, Moses writes a song as a witness against the people and attaches it to the close of this book (Deut. 32). Though the song leaves little doubt that Israel's immediate future will be no different than its imperfect past, the book closes by directing the reader's attention to a time in the more distant future—a time when a "prophet . . . like Moses" (34:10) will come and lead the people to obey God's will. This will be the days of the new covenant (Jer. 31:31–34; Ezek. 36:24–28).

Joshua

The book of Joshua shows that the Lord did, in fact, fulfill his promises to Abraham (Gen. 13:15) and Moses (Ex. 3:8) in giving Israel the Promised Land. Thus, this book is a lesson on the *faithfulness of God* and his promises (cf. Josh. 21:43–45; 23:14). At the same time, however, the book sets the stage for the beginning of a new era in God's dealings with Israel—namely, the history of *Israel's failure* to trust God and live up to their covenant obligations as his people (cf. 23:15–16). This had already characterized Israel's past history recorded in the Pentateuch and characterizes the historical books that follow.

(1) God manifests his faithfulness in three ways in the narratives of Joshua. (a) In the numerous accounts of Israel's successful conquest of the land (Josh. 1–12). The author shows Joshua's amazing success was a result of his following God's law. After receiving God's command to meditate daily on his Word, Joshua began to conquer the land successfully. He conquered Jericho first (chs. 1–6), then Ai (chs. 7–8; Ai was taken only after Israel's hidden sin was dealt with). Israel then took the land of "all the kings west of the Jordan," and God continued to deliver the Canaanites into their hands (chs. 9–12).

(b) In the detailed lists of territory taken and occupied by various tribes (Josh. 13–22). The book records the allotment of the land east of the Jordan River (ch. 13) and west (chs. 14–19), including the appointment of the cities of refuge (ch. 20) and the Levitical cities (ch. 21).

(c) In summary statements placed strategically throughout the book. One of these is Joshua 21:43–45, which emphasizes God's fulfillment of his promises through Joshua: "So the LORD gave Israel all the land he had sworn to give their forefathers, and they took possession of it and settled there. . . . Not one of all the LORD's good promises to the house of Israel failed; every one was fulfilled."

(2) At the end of the book (Josh. 23:15), however, we begin to hear more distinctly the note of Israel's failure, "But just as every good promise of the LORD your God has come true, so the LORD will bring on you all the evil he has threatened, until he has destroyed you from this good land he has given you."

The man Joshua is a model of godly leadership. Not only are we prepared by the Pentateuchal narratives to accept his leadership as a replacement of Moses (Num. 27:18–23), but even more, we are repeatedly reminded that his leadership was characterized by the work of God's Spirit (Num. 27:18; Deut. 34:9; cf. Num. 11:16–30). In Joshua, whose name means "deliverer," we see a picture of someone who would some day come and deliver his people from their sins—the One who himself was named "the Deliverer," that is, Jesus (Matt. 1:21).

Judges

The close similarity between the judges and the later Israelite kings provides the basic motif of the book of Judges. After Joshua's death, Israel was without a godly leader. Thus the only leadership that remained in Israel was vested in the office of the judge. The Lord raised up special leaders as his personal representatives to fill that office and to instruct the people in God's Torah (Judg. 2:16–19).

Some of the judges were raised up by God to meet emergency situations and to provide heroic military leadership. Samson, for example, seems to have provided little else than this. But other judges were raised up as life-long teachers of God's law (Judg. 10:1–5; 12:8–15), providing strong leadership for the needs of the nation. The judge thus served as a model or paradigm of God's leadership among his people. When the people trusted God, God raised up a judge to lead them against their enemies.

Why did the writer of this book recount the events of the lives of some judges but pass over others? He seems particularly interested in those judges who exercised (1) military leadership against God's enemies and (2) covenant leadership with God's people. They were able to save the people only when they obeyed God's will in the covenant. These judges—Othniel, Ehud, Deborah, Gideon, Jephthah, and Samson—most closely resembled the kind of king Israel should have. They were the best models of godly leadership—not because they were especially godly men and women in every respect, but because they were men and women who saw themselves as instruments in God's hands.

Two central lessons are found in the book of Judges: (1) The welfare of the nation depended directly on a knowledge of God's will, the Torah; (2) God would punish his people for their unfaithfulness to his covenant. The book begins (Judg. 2) with negative examples of these lessons, and the lack of godly leadership in Israel is graphically portrayed in the stories at the conclusion of the book (chs. 17–21).

Ruth

This book opens with an account of God's people in exile. They are in the land of Moab in the days of the judges because of a famine in the land. The story of Ruth thus begins with a typical, but most impossible, situation. Through the events of the story, God took this seemingly hopeless situation and turned it to his purpose and glory by finding a single faithful Moabite woman, Ruth, who had married into the house of Judah. This is a most unlikely beginning to a story about the coming of the promised seed of the line of David.

When Naomi returned to the land of Israel, her daughter-in-law Ruth accompanied her. The latter's faithfulness and trust in God were well known throughout the whole region (Ruth 2:11), and God was about to repay Ruth for her faithfulness (2:12). The first fruits of God's blessing came in the form of Boaz's special treatment of her and his provision for her family (2:13–18). As Naomi said, God was behind all these events: "He has not stopped showing his kindness to the living and the dead" (2:20). Though within the story these words have the immediate sense of God's care for her as a widow and her family, within the larger context of the book her words take on a greater significance that relates to God's promises to the house of Judah (cf. Gen. 49:8–12), specifically, to David (cf. Ruth 4:22; 2 Sam. 7:16).

The law of the levirate marriage apparently lies behind the story of Ruth's night visit to Boaz (see Deut. 25:5–10; cf. Gen. 38:8). Naomi suggested to Ruth that she force the hand of Boaz in obtaining for their family the right of inheritance. This was an important step in God's faithfulness in establishing the house of David. That is, behind these plans and schemes lies the faithfulness of a providential God, working out his eternal plans.

The story closes with the details of the actual transaction (Ruth 4:1–12). The closest relative forfeits his right to Ruth's inheritance (4:1–6). Up to this point in the story the recurring theme has been God's faithfulness in establishing the house of David and the confluence of human events to that purpose. Therefore when the closest relative refuses to buy Ruth's inheritance and take her as his wife, we see further evidence of God's providence.

The words of the elders and city leaders express the central theme of the book: "May the LORD make the woman who is coming into your home like Rachel and Leah" (Ruth 4:11). They help draw a line connecting those promises with the house of Judah, "Through the offspring the LORD gives you by this young woman, may your family be like that of Perez, whom Tamar bore to Judah" (4:12). The genealogy at the conclusion of the book makes the final link between this story and the birth of David—as well as the Son of David, the Messiah.

1 Samuel

Like Samson who preceded him as Israel's judge, Samuel was chosen for his service even before he was born (1 Sam. 1:11). His birth held a hint of the central role he would play in establishing the Davidic kingship and the messianic promise, for Hannah announced that God would "give strength to his king and exalt the horn of his anointed" (2:10). During Samuel's early years as a prophet and judge, Israel faced some of its darkest days—the ark of the covenant was captured by the Philistines and Israel was overrun by their conquerors (4:1–11; 7:14).

During this tenure Samuel was able to rally the people to renew their trust in the Lord and, as the judges who had preceded him, to deliver Israel from its foreign oppressors—the Philistines (1 Sam. 7:3–13). At the close of his life, however, the people requested him to appoint a king over them to rule, just as the other nations had (8:4–5). Rather than wait for God to raise up another judge, the people wanted a permanent leader, a king. At the Lord's urging, Samuel acquiesced to their plan and established the kingship in Israel with the house of Saul.

Saul (whose name means "the one [you] asked for") failed as king because he did not provide spiritual leadership for the nation. He overstepped his bounds within God's established pattern for the king—he did not heed the words of God spoken by the prophet (1 Sam. 13:9–14). As it turned out, Saul was the kind of king Israel had wanted in that he maintained a standing army, but he was not the kind of king the Lord wanted, for he did not obey God's will (Deut. 18:15). Thus, Saul was rejected as king and ultimately died in battle (1 Sam. 31:4). But after his rejection as king, he was not immediately removed from the scene. Instead he remained to provide a vivid contrast with David, the newly appointed king and a man after God's own heart.

As the youngest son of Jesse, of the tribe of Judah, David was the second and most successful king of Israel. Under him the Israelite nation reached its highest level both spiritually and politically (see 2 Samuel). The second half of this book outlines the courage and sincerity of David's heart (1 Sam. 16–31). We follow him in military conquests, in flight from Saul, and in dealings with the people of Israel. David's descendants ruled the southern kingdom of Judah until the Babylonian exile. The New Testament refers to David fifty-eight times, many of which mention that Jesus Christ was a direct descendant and the rightful heir to the throne (cf. Matt. 1).

2 Samuel

The book of 2 Samuel can be entitled, "The Rise and Fall of King David." The writer portrays David as an ideal king, but not the "ideal king" that the biblical writers had longed for (cf. Gen. 49:10). The point of these narratives is to show that when the ideal king comes, he will be like David, his ancestor, but that David himself was not the Promised One. Israel must still look into the future, waiting for the coming of the Messiah.

The writer first traces David's rise to power and recognition among all the Israelites (2 Sam. 1–5). He captured the city of Jerusalem (ch. 5) and brought the ark of the covenant to its resting place there (ch. 6). While preparing to build a temple in Jerusalem, God sent the prophet Nathan to tell him that he would not build a "house" (i.e., a temple) for God; rather, God would build a "house" (i.e., a dynasty) for David. God thus promised the house of David that a descendant would come from his loins who would build a house for God in Jerusalem and establish an eternal kingdom (ch. 7). To the reader of 2 Samuel, God's promise could be referring to any one of David's sons. The narrative brings them all before the reader, one by one, showing their deeds and manner of life. But there is little doubt at the close of the book that none of his sons was the intended fulfillment of God's promise.

One son remained, however—the son of Bathsheba, Solomon. Was he perhaps the son whom God promised? The book of 2 Samuel does not answer that question (see 1 Kings); it is content to show that neither David himself (chs. 8–12), nor his sons Amnon (chs. 13–14) and Absalom (chs. 15–20), fulfilled the promise. At the end of his life, however, David's hope remained undaunted. He wrote psalms and sang praises to God in hope of his promise. The book of Psalms is full of them—one of which is included at the close of 2 Samuel (ch. 22; see Ps. 18). David praises God for showing "unfailing kindness to his Messiah [NIV: anointed], to David and his descendants forever" (2 Sam. 22:51). Attached to the end of this psalm are "the last words of David" (23:1–7), in which he again reaffirms his trust in God's "everlasting covenant" (23:5).

The book closes on the somber note: David's last years were spent in futile attempts to garner his own protection through building a mighty army and surrounding himself with great warriors (2 Sam. 23–24). Nevertheless, his final act—that of purchasing the site of the future temple (ch. 24)—prepared for the fulfillment of God's promise to build his temple in Jerusalem.

1 Kings

The book of 1 Kings picks up immediately from 2 Samuel with the question of who would succeed David as king. Would it be Adonijah or Solomon? The question was important because it raised the possibility that either of these two sons might be the heir to the divine promises of 2 Samuel 7. As events turned out, Solomon was anointed king (1 Kings 1–2). Immediately he set out consciously to fulfill the Davidic promise. He prayed for wisdom (chs. 3–4) and built the temple (chs. 5–9)—two features of the ideal king envisioned in 2 Samuel 7 and 23. Indeed, in recounting the story of Solomon, the writer seems intent on leading us into believing that Solomon was the Promised One. Solomon even saw himself as that seed (1 Kings 5:5), and we are on the verge of accepting his word as the final verdict.

But then we learn that Solomon was not the seed promised by God. The conditions for the fulfillment of God's promise to David were reiterated to Solomon: "As for this temple you are building, if you follow my decrees, carry out my regulations and keep all my commands and obey them, I will fulfill through you the promise I gave to David your father" (6:12). By the time the story is complete, we know that Solomon did not meet these conditions (11:9–13).

Thus, within the flow of the narrative, we are redirected to look far beyond the immediate descendants of David for the fulfillment of the promise. It is in this sense that 1 (and 2) Kings are messianic. They develop the theme of the promised seed of David and show that none of the historical kings in the house of David met the conditions of obedience to the will of God that was to characterize the promised Messiah. The writer also wants us to see Solomon's work on the temple as a picture or image of the ultimate fulfillment of God's promise to David. The Promised Seed would be like Solomon.

After Solomon's death, his kingdom was divided—the result of a foolish decision of the young king Rehoboam. The northern tribes rebelled against the Davidic dynasty in Jerusalem and established an independent kingdom. Jeroboam son of Nebat, from the tribe of Ephraim, who had once rebelled against Solomon (1 Kings 11:26), was chosen as king (12:20).

The remainder of the book shows both the increasing wickedness of the Israelite and Judean kings and the role of the prophets in confronting them. As he had promised in Deuteronomy 18:15–18, God raised up his servants the prophets, who challenged the apostasy of the kings. Elijah was the key prophet throughout these narratives. His courage managed to keep the office of the prophet alive during these dark years.

2 Kings

The division between 1 and 2 Kings came only late in the history of the Bible; in reality the two books are one. Thus, 2 Kings continues with the same plan and purpose as 1 Kings. Although kings and prophets came and went, God continued to work among his people. But God did not withhold his judgment forever, for the rebellious kingdoms were eventually punished. Behind the scenes of apostasy and confusion depicted in this book stood a patient and long-suffering God (cf. Ex. 34:6), not willing that any should perish but that all might come to repentance. God only reluctantly brought punishment on his people.

In the strategy of 2 Kings, the prophet Elisha replaced Elijah as God's instrument, confronting the rebellious kings with the call to repentance and obedience (2 Kings 1–13). When Elisha asked Elijah for a "double portion of your spirit" (2:9b) he was not only asking to continue the work of Elijah but to increase it as well. To show that his wish was granted, the writer selected the narratives about Elijah and Elisha so that there are twice as many miracles recorded for Elisha (eight for Elijah, sixteen for Elisha).

The writer of 2 Kings relentlessly reminds his readers that the kings of the northern kingdom (Israel) continued to lead the people in the "sin of Jeroboam," that is, the establishment of worship centers apart from the temple in Jerusalem. Though modern readers may find no harm in such a practice, to the biblical writer this meant a stubborn refusal to acknowledge the supremacy of God's will. God was to be worshiped when, where, and how he willed (Deut. 12). Israel's disobedience resulted in exile. After a long siege of Israel's capital city, Samaria, and a wholesale invasion of the land, the Assyrians captured the city and sent the Israelites into exile.

The rest of 2 Kings records the final events in the reign of the Davidic kings of Judah. Though there were temporary reforms under Hezekiah (2 Kings 18–20) and Josiah (chs. 22–23), the kingdom of Judah was eventually invaded by the Babylonian king, Nebuchadnezzar (24:1); Jerusalem was destroyed, and the people were taken into exile. These things happened to Judah because they failed to obey God's word, just as the prophets had foretold (24:3). The fulfillment of God's word is a central theme of the book.

The judgment of the exile is not the last word in this book, however. There was still hope in God's promises to the house of David because it was an eternal promise (2 Sam. 7:16). Thus, at the close of this book, the writer notes that the house of David was not only still intact but even flourishing in the house of the king of Babylon (2 Kings 25:28). There was still hope for the fulfillment of God's promise to David.

1 Chronicles

The book of 1 Chronicles is intended as a commentary on the early portions of the Old Testament, particularly 1 and 2 Samuel. The author did not want merely to retell the story of those earlier books. Rather, he wanted to recast those stories so that their meaning could be made more clear to his own and future generations. He was particularly interested in bringing out the importance of God's promise to David in 2 Samuel 7, in which God declared that the age-old promise of a Redeemer, a Messiah, would be fulfilled in the house and lineage of David.

This book begins with the first man, Adam, and traces especially the lineage of David, showing how he fulfilled the hope of God's people and how his descendants carried with them that same hope (1 Chron. 1–8). Giving only scant attention to Saul (chs. 9–10), the author discusses the rise of the kingdom of David (chs. 11–16), focusing particularly on his concern for the ark of the covenant (chs. 13–16). David's rise to power was synonymous with the ark's transport to Jerusalem, because the author believed the role of the king was closely related to that of a priest (he shares this hope with his contemporary, the prophet Zechariah [cf. Zech. 6:9–15]). David's kingship was like that of Melchizedek (Gen. 14:18), just as the Messiah's would be (cf. Ps. 110:4).

This perspective comes out clearly in the author's retelling of the Davidic covenant of 2 Samuel 7, where God had made a promise of an eternal King to arise out of the house of David. In 1 Chronicles 17:14 God said, "I will set him over my house and my kingdom forever." When God said "my house," he meant "my temple." Thus the Promised Scion of the house of David would carry out the duties of both a priest and a king.

Appropriately, then, 1 Chronicles shows extensively David's concern for the temple and the worship of God carried out there. While David himself could not build the temple since he was a man of war (1 Chron. 18–21) and had shed too much blood (22:8), his preparations for the temple were so comprehensive that they left little for his son and successor to do. The remainder of 1 Chronicles, after the account of the Davidic covenant and David's wars, recounts the work that he did to prepare for building the temple—gathering the materials (ch. 22); appointing the Levites (ch. 23), priests (ch. 24), singers (ch. 25), gatekeepers (26:1–19), and officials (26:20–32); and laying out the plans (chs. 28–29).

The books of Chronicles are found at the end of the Hebrew Bible. They thus provide a fitting bridge to the coming of the Messiah in the New Testament.

2 Chronicles

The book of 2 Chronicles begins with the kingship of Solomon. Like his father David, Solomon's activities were devoted to building and dedicating the temple. He was thus a fitting symbol of the King who was still yet to come, that promised Messiah from the house of David. Although Solomon was not the Promised One, his reign closely approximated the reign of that coming King. In keeping with this "messianic symbolism," the writer emphasizes how Solomon was known throughout the ancient world for his wisdom. Thus, his reign ends with the visit from the Queen of Sheba, showing that the report of Solomon's wisdom had reached the ends of the earth. This is the same picture of Solomon (and the Messiah) that is exemplified in Psalm 72.

The books of 1 and 2 Chronicles were written long after the downfall of the house of David and were not intended to be understood as merely extolling the glories of the past. They were written to enliven the hope of the people in God's promise to David and thus to strengthen their faith in the coming King. In keeping with this concern, the author devotes the last chapters of his book to the history of the Davidic dynasty. After Solomon's reign, the kingdom built by David all but fell to ruin, and no descendant could rightly claim to be the fulfillment of God's promise to David. There were revivals in which godly kings did their best to lead the people in obedience to God's Word, but they all ended in failure. The reader's hope is directed to the fulfillment of a promise not yet realized.

Solomon's son Rehoboam began his reign with a crisis that left the house of David in control of only the tribe of Judah; the rest of David's kingdom lay in the hands of Solomon's rival, Jeroboam. Because that kingdom lay outside the province of the Davidic dynasty, the author bypasses most of its history in favor of a more detailed treatment of the southern kingdom, Judah. He tells the history of Judah to its conclusion and ruin in the Babylonian captivity. This book ends with the edict of the Persian king Cyrus, issuing a call to rebuild the temple in Jerusalem. The author remains focused on the temple and the Promised One who would one day rebuild it. The last words of the book, "Let him go up," become a call for the return of the Messiah, resembling the last words of the New Testament, "Come, Lord Jesus."

The books of Chronicles are found at the end of the Hebrew Bible. They thus provide a fitting bridge to the coming of the Messiah in the New Testament.

Ezra

The book of Ezra begins with a fulfilled prophecy from the book of Jeremiah. Jeremiah had foretold that Judah would go into exile to Babylon (Jer. 25:8–10) and that this exile would last seventy years (25:11), after which time Judah would return to the land (29:10–14). The writer of Ezra, referring to that prophecy, sees a fulfillment in the first group of Jews who returned to Jerusalem under the leadership of Zerubbabel and Joshua the high priest (Ezra 1–6).

The primary task of that first group was to reconstruct the temple. The people celebrated with the laying of the foundation (Ezra 3:10–11). Those who had seen the former temple, the one built by Solomon, wept in sorrow, while others shouted for joy (3:12–13). Already Solomon's temple was being idealized. Though there was joy in what God had done in the present, there was still room for hope that greater blessings would come. Part of this book's strategy is to show that the ultimate fulfillment of God's promises remained in the future.

All these events were the result of the sovereign work of God. He had "stirred up the heart" (Ezra 1:1; NIV: "moved the heart") of Cyrus to allow the Jews to return; and he had "stirred up the heart" (1:5; NIV: "moved the heart") of the people to leave Babylon and return to Jerusalem to build the temple.

All was not well, however. There were two distinct signs of trouble. (1) When Zerubbabel and those working on the temple refused to allow the local inhabitants of the land to participate in the building, "counselors" were hired "to frustrate their plans," thus effectively halting the work on the temple throughout the reign of Cyrus and into the reign of the next king, Darius (Ezra 4:4–5, 24; 5:16b). After a long delay, the temple reconstruction resumed, and it was completed in the sixth year of Darius (6:13–15). The Levitical priesthood was installed during an elaborate dedication of the temple (6:16–18), and in the same year the people celebrated the Passover with great joy (6:19–22).

(2) Several decades after the rebuilding, Ezra the scribe returned to Jerusalem from Babylonian exile. He was a priest of the house of Aaron (Ezra 7:1–5) and was "well versed in the Law of Moses" (7:6). The major problem he faced was that the people, and especially their leaders, had "not kept themselves separate from the neighboring peoples with their detestable practices" (9:1). They had not obeyed the law of Moses. Although the problem involved intermarriage (9:2) of their sons to the daughters of the nations, the real difficulty lay with their "unfaithfulness" to God (9:3–4). Through Ezra's faithful prayer of repentance (ch. 9), the people turned to God and obeyed his law (ch. 10). Through his example, the book teaches the importance of prayer and repentance in the life of God's people.

Nehemiah

The book of Nehemiah opens with godly Nehemiah hearing of the despicable condition of the city of Jerusalem (Neh. 1:1–4). The walls lay in ruin and the gates were torn down. Because he held a high office in the court of the Persian king Artaxerxes I, Nehemiah was able to do something about it— though not without the Lord's help. He went immediately to prayer (1:5–11), confessing the sins of his fathers as well as his own. Throughout his prayer, there was also a clear sense of hope. Just as God had been faithful to his covenant promises when he brought judgment on the nation, so there was the hope that he would also remain true to his promises and bring salvation and blessing. The basis of Nehemiah's hope was God's promise in Deuteronomy 30, which he paraphrased in this prayer: "When you and your children return to the LORD your God and obey him with all your heart and with all your soul according to everything I command you today, then the LORD your God will restore your fortunes" (Deut. 30:2–3).

Having obtained permission and assistance from Artaxerxes I to return and rebuild the city of Jerusalem, Nehemiah began his journey. As the rebuilding of the wall began (Neh. 2:17–18), opposition immediately arose (2:19–20); the people were mocked and taunted by their enemies. Nehemiah met each case of opposition by trusting God and striving to be obedient to God's word. In fifty-two days the wall was completed.

On the first day of the seventh month, Ezra stood on a high wooden platform and read aloud the "Book of the Law of Moses" (Neh. 8:1). This was a special day of rest (Sabbath), the Feast of Trumpets (Lev. 23:23–25; Num. 29:1–6). Another special day of fasting and repentance was called on the twenty-fourth day of the same month (Neh. 9:1). The Israelites "separated themselves from all foreigners . . . stood in their places and confessed their sins and the wickedness of their fathers" (9:2). The writer of Nehemiah suggests that by now the people had reached the same state of repentance and godly sorrow as Nehemiah had at the beginning of the book (cf. 1:4–11). The people bound themselves "with a curse and an oath to follow the Law of God given through Moses the servant of God and to obey carefully all the commands, regulations and decrees of the LORD our Lord" (10:29).

The book concludes with a personal account of Nehemiah's additional reforms (Neh. 13). The historical return from exile was a part of God's plan of blessing for his people, but it was not the last word in that plan. Though God had remained faithful, the people again failed to trust and obey him. The book thus looks beyond the immediate present and forward to still another time in the future when God would fulfill his promises to Israel and the people would respond in faith.

Esther

The story of Esther is similar to the stories of Joseph (Gen. 37–50), Moses (Ex. 2), David (1 Sam. 29–30), Daniel (Daniel), and Nehemiah (Nehemiah). In each of these, a gifted Israelite is taken into the palace of a foreign king and granted an opportunity to preserve the life of God's people. Each story makes its own contribution to the larger question of God's providential care for his people.

The book of Esther teaches this lesson without ever mentioning God. He remains the unspoken "actor" in an otherwise entirely human drama. To say it another way, God is not so much an implied actor in the drama as he is the author of the script. The emphasis is thus on divine providence. Given the series of "coincidences" at key moments in the story, the reader knows that the events happened as they did because God planned them that way. Mordecai says as much in his challenge to Esther at the peak of the story: "Who knows but that you have come to royal position for such a time as this?" (Est. 4:14).

The story begins with a royal banquet given by the Persian King Xerxes (Est. 1:1–9), during which Queen Vashti refused the king's request to attend his banquet and thus forfeited her claim to the throne (1:10–22). Ironically, the king, in his search for a queen who would obey him (2:1–4), found Esther (2:5–18), who had the courage to disobey him at a moment of crisis (4:10–11; 5:1–2).

Mordecai's refusal to bow before Haman incited him against the Jews (Est. 3:1–15). It is not hard to see in that refusal a parallel to the equally bold refusal of Shadrach, Meshach, and Abednego to bow down to Nebuchadnezzar's golden image (Dan. 3:16–18), or Daniel's continued daily prayers in the face of Darius' prohibition (6:10). Each case shows a willingness to accept the consequences and implies a confidence that God would intervene.

Mordecai's initial response to Haman's decree did not reveal the underlying stratagem that later surfaced. He was simply overwhelmed with grief and horror (Est. 4:1–5). In his pleading with Esther to confront the king, however, we see the well-laid plans of a wise counselor (4:6–17). Mordecai's words to Esther focus the reader's attention on the central lesson of the book: "If you remain silent at this time, relief and deliverance for the Jews will arise from another place" (4:14). Though God's plans depend on human efforts, they are not limited by them. Human decisions are only the means by which something becomes a part of God's plans. Esther chose to go before the king and become a part of God's plan for his people.

Job

This book tells the story of Job, a perfectly wise man. The Lord himself describes him as "blameless and upright, a man who fears God and shuns evil" (Job 1:8). As such Job becomes the target of Satan's challenge.

As the story progresses, Job learns deeper lessons about God and a human being's relationship to him: true wisdom and true godliness come from complete submission to God's rule, regardless of temporary rewards or suffering. Job echoes this conclusion in the final scene of the book: "I know that you can do all things; no plan of yours can be thwarted. . . . My ears had heard of you but now my eyes have seen you. Therefore I retract [NIV: despise myself] and repent in dust and ashes" (Job 42:2–6). Job repents of his own imposition of limitations on God's sovereign will as well as the limitations he had placed on God's authority: "Surely I spoke of things I did not understand, things too wonderful for me to know" (42:3).

Job's three friends each make the point that no one, including Job, is free from sin and thus inherently righteous before God. They also hold, in agreement with the rest of Scripture, that God punishes sin. Thus each one concludes that Job ought to examine his life more carefully to see what sin or sins may be the cause of his troubles. Their advice is always the same: "If you return to the Almighty you will be restored" (Job 22:23; cf. 5:8–17; 8:20; 11:13–15; 22:21–30; 36:8–11). We as readers know their advice is good but misplaced. We are relieved when Elihu comes on the scene to square matters with Job.

According to Elihu, Job's troubles are to be understood as divine discipline and instruction. Human beings cannot, of course, question God's justice (Job 34:16). But Job's problems may be explained by other means than by assuming that Job has sinned (33:13–30), for God may allow misfortune in someone's life to correct that person or to keep him or her from foolish pride. Job's only safe response is "to fear" the Lord and trust his justice (37:23–24).

There is still more to the issue. We must listen to God's final words (Job 38–41) and then to the words of the author in the epilogue (ch. 42). We can then see the events from the divine perspective. Since human beings do not have all the resources to question God's justice, the truly wise person submits to God's will. When God's people do so, they can expect the eventual return of divine blessing.

Psalms

The book of Psalms can be read as a single book, with each individual psalm intentionally arranged within the book in a meaningful way. The underlying arrangement of these songs encourages us to view them as pointing to the Messiah.

The first psalm introduces the book as a whole. It establishes the central theme—meditation on Scripture is the way the righteous know God's will. In God's written word, the righteous find blessing; those who reject it are the wicked, and they will perish in the day of judgment.

The second psalm is attached to the first as a means of further qualifying this central theme. This psalm is a messianic one, based on the promise to David in 2 Samuel 7:16. It depicts the hope of God's fulfilling his promise to David by sending a victorious king to rule over Israel and the nations. By attaching this psalm to the first psalm, the author shows that meditation on Scripture ultimately leads to trusting in the Messiah (Ps. 2:12). As Jesus said, "If you believed Moses, you would believe me, for he wrote about me" (John 5:46).

These two psalms set the agenda and define the central theme of the rest of the psalms. The strategy of the arrangement relies on a number of editorial features, some as simple as the sequence of the psalms themselves. The superscriptions play an important role in the overall interpretation of the psalms. In Psalm 3, for example, the superscription states that this psalm represents the words of David "when he fled from his son Absalom." That comment clarifies that the psalms intentionally follow the order of the book of 2 Samuel. God first made a promise to David regarding his son (2 Sam. 7 = Ps. 2), and then the rebellion of his son Absalom is narrated (2 Sam. 15 = Ps. 3). Both texts raise the same question: How can the Messiah come from the sons of David (e.g., Absalom, Adonijah, Solomon) if they have proved faithless and rebellious? The answer is clear enough. God has promised a future Son of David, the Messiah.

Both 2 Samuel and the book of Psalms show David's confidence and faith in God's promise, even in the face of the failure of his own household to live up to the expectations of that promise. Second Samuel does this by narrating the events in David's life that show his confidence in God's promise; Psalms does this by recounting the words of David's prayers and praise, especially his assurance and hope in the coming Messiah. Thanks to the superscriptions, we see that although these psalms are the words of David and recount incidents in his life, they are, in fact, about the Messiah and David's assurance of God's faithfulness to send him.

Proverbs

The purpose of the book of Proverbs is "attaining wisdom and discipline . . . giving prudence to the simple, knowledge and discretion to the young" (Prov. 1:2–4). The person addressed in the book is called "son," and the counsel given is referred to as "your father's instruction" and "your mother's teaching" (1:8).

In his defense of divine wisdom, the writer turns first to the dangers of the evil influence of sinners and the devastating effect they can have on the young. Turning then to the metaphor of wisdom as a woman, the writer speaks of her crying aloud in the streets. She is a mother seeking her wayward son or a wife calling out to her unfaithful husband. She is looking for him in the very streets and public squares where he abandoned her. By contrast, finding wisdom is like finding a virtuous wife. Such wisdom God himself possessed in creating the universe, and he rewards those who have it.

With these exhortations and examples as a backdrop, the book opens up into the full array of Solomonic proverbs (Prov. 10–24). They cover the whole range of human life and all levels of human social activities: relationships between family members, business partners, neighbors, friends, and enemies. Within these proverbs are two distinct groups. The first consists of short, single line sayings (Prov. 10:1–22:29); the second (23:1–24:22) expands the sayings by introducing a new dimension into the discussion of wisdom—divine judgment and future punishment. Here wisdom has been brought into the arena of divine revelation. This is not just good advice for the here and now, it is eternal advice.

A further collection of Solomon's wise sayings was gathered by court officials during the reign of King Hezekiah (Prov. 25:1) and added to the book (chs. 25–29). The content of nearly all these sayings relates to political rule or governance, though the application of these principles applies to private life as well. One could entitle this section, "Principles of Leadership."

The book of Proverbs has little recognizable structure to aid in the interpretation of each saying. Consequently, the reader must understand each saying apart from any literary context. In seeking an appropriate context we must search within the context of our own life for an application. Perhaps for just this reason the author of Proverbs closes the book with a close-up account of three individuals, Agur (Prov. 30:1–33), Lemuel (31:1–9), and "wife of noble character" (31:10–31), in which we see wisdom through the lens of their lives. They become the model for the reader's own life-application of wisdom.

Ecclesiastes

The *preacher* ("Ecclesiastes"; NIV teacher) is the primary character of this book. Though not expressly stated, he is probably meant to be identified as Solomon, "son of David, king in Jerusalem" (Eccl. 1:1). At the close of the book, the *author* (or narrator) cuts into the preacher's monologue and brings the book to its conclusion (12:9–14).

It is important to note that in these final remarks, the author stands somewhat in critical judgment over the words of the preacher, both evaluating them and attempting to see them in a larger context. From his standpoint, the preacher's words are wise words, "upright and true" (12:9–10), and as such are like those of other wise men (12:11); but taken in themselves, they do not state the whole of the matter. They are truth, but not the whole truth. The author has become weary in seeking out wisdom from the books of the wise, such as those of the preacher (12:12). According to him, the simple truth to live by is to "fear God and keep his commandments, for this is the whole duty of man. For God will bring every deed into judgment" (12:13–14).

In other words, human wisdom has its limits. In the end, only God's commandments as revealed in Scripture can find ultimate reward. Thus the viewpoint expressed by the author, as opposed to the preacher himself, is the same as that of Moses in Deuteronomy 4:6. There Moses identified the Torah, God's Word, with wisdom, "For this [the Torah] will show your wisdom."

It is important to keep the author's perspective in mind in understanding the message of this book, for the author does not always agree with what the preacher says. To put it another way, the author often records the words of the preacher and then adds his own qualification to them. The preacher's words are presented as conclusions drawn from the point of view of human wisdom, but they are not the last word. The final word is always God's perspective.

For example, the preacher says, "Man's fate is like that of the animals; the same fate awaits them both: As one dies, so dies the other. . . . man has no advantage over the animal. Everything is meaningless" (Eccl. 3:19). The author, however, has prefaced these words with the more general statement that "God will bring to judgment both the righteous and the wicked, for there will be a time [of judgment] for every activity, a time [of judgment] for every deed" (3:17). This considerably softens the words of the preacher. While the preacher may be speaking as a wise man who views the world around him with all the limitations of human existence (3:19), the author adds the divine perspective on judgment and eternal reward for the righteous (3:17).

Song of Songs

This book expresses Solomon's love for a young woman. Its straightforward depiction of human love in all its aspects has given rise to various figurative interpretations at every stage in its history. Jewish interpreters understand it as a picture of God's relationship to his beloved Israel, whereas Christians have commonly understood it in terms of Christ and his church. In modern times many interpreters of the book have understood it "literally," as an ode to human love. To suggest, however, that this drama of two lovers is the primary intent of the book is to confuse the poetic imagery with the purpose of the poem.

We here offer a new understanding of the Song of Songs. We suggest it be read as an expression of Israel's messianic hope. Internal clues in the book itself suggests that it was intended as a portrait of the Messiah's love for divine wisdom. The Messiah is pictured as Solomon, and, as in the book of Proverbs, "wisdom" is personified as the young and beautiful woman. What is said here of the young woman closely parallels what is said about wisdom in Proverbs. Throughout the poem the notion of love is idealized insofar as its obtainment lies in the future. This is not a love poem; it is a poem about love.

One's interpretation of the Song of Songs turns on the statements about the young woman at the end of the book. According to the beloved, the quest for wisdom was aroused "under the apple tree" (Song 8:4a). This is probably an allusion to the Garden of Eden when the first woman "saw that the fruit of the tree was ... desirable for gaining wisdom [and] she took some and ate it" (Gen. 3:6). Thus the desire for wisdom was aroused but not gratified. The full obtainment of wisdom will come only when the Messiah, like Solomon in this poem, comes to claim his beloved.

If this interpretation is correct and the phrase "under the apple tree" refers to the "tree of the knowledge of good and evil" in Genesis 2–3, then the reference to "there your mother conceived you, there she who was in labor gave you birth" (Song 8:5b) suggests that the author of this song also understood both the promised "seed" in Genesis 3:15 and the reference to Eve as "the mother of all the living" (3:20) messianically. Such a link places this song on a different level than that of an ode to human love, gives credence to traditional attempts to see more in this poem than meets the eye, and provides guidelines along which the symbolism is to be read.

Reading the Song of Songs in this manner provides insight into the underlying justification for its inclusion into the canon of the Old Testament. Most recognize today that the time of the formation of the Old Testament canon coincided with a significant surge in the hope of the imminent return of the messianic King. The book was included in the canon, one might say, because it was seen as a picture of the Messiah.

The Prophetic Literature

Classification of the Prophetic Literature

Major Prophets	Minor Prophets			
Isaiah	Hosea	Joel	Amos	Obadiah
Jeremiah	Jonah	Micah	Nahum	Habakkuk
Ezekiel	Zephaniah	Haggar	Zechariah	Malachi

Preexilic Prophets	Exilic Prophets	Postexilic Prophets
Isaiah	Ezekiel	Haggai
Jeremiah	Daniel	Zechariah
Hosea		Malachi
Zephaniah		

The last seventeen books of the Old Testament form the prophetic literature. The prophets, spanning three and one-half centuries, were messengers of the covenant God. Sent to a disobedient people, they were not innovators but revivalists, calling the people back to the faith of their fathers, the faith of the covenant promises to Abraham, Moses, and David.

During the time of the prophets, the people of the covenant had fallen away from God and his covenant and were failing to keep its commands. But Israel did not realize that they were living in apostasy. They had mistaken the blessings of the covenant (God's presence at the temple) for the requirements of the covenant (their own obedience). Rather than return to the Lord in repentance and obedience, the people presumed upon God's presence among them, saying, "Is not the LORD among us? No disaster will come upon us" (Mic. 3:11; cf. Jer. 7:1–7).

In the face of such false security, the prophets bring the startling word that God is not on the side of his own covenant people. They have forsaken his covenant, and now he is to send judgment on them. A dominant theme, then, in the prophets is divine judgment: One day all of Israel's objects of comfort and religious support will be taken away, and God will judge them for their disobedience (Isa. 3:1–8). He will pour out his wrath on his own people.

Interwoven in these themes of divine wrath and judgment, however, are many strands of a counter-theme, the theme of divine blessing and salvation. God promised "the fathers" long ago that through their seed would come blessing to all humanity (Gen. 12:2–3). Thus, in spite of the imminent judgment about to fall on the people, there is yet hope for the future. Many texts throughout the prophetic literature speak of this hope of salvation in the midst of judgment, the most important of which are Isaiah 4:2–6; 9:2–7; Jeremiah 31:31ff.; Ezekiel 36:22–28; Hosea 1:8–2:2; Micah 7:18–20.

Isaiah

The opening section of Isaiah (Isa. 1–2) is a microcosm of the rest of the book. Israel, God's own people, have forsaken him and thus stand in danger of divine wrath. Interwoven into this theme of judgment is the equally important theme of salvation and God's faithfulness. Jerusalem will be left desolate, but a remnant will survive. In the future, the "last days," Jerusalem will again be the center of God's work among the nations. Those nations will stream into the holy city and learn God's will instead of the ways of war. At that time God will judge all the nations and punish them for trusting in their idols. Divine wrath will come even on God's people in Jerusalem and Judah, but God will also send a Savior, the Messiah.

In Isaiah's own day, the rise of the Assyrian Empire is seen as an act of God, preparing an instrument of wrath against his disobedient people (Isa. 7:17). The time when God punishes the nations and brings peace to Israel involves not only the Assyrians but all the nations of the world (chs. 13–35). In that day, there will be a righteous king in Jerusalem (32:1); he will be the Messiah.

The Judean king, Hezekiah, is a model of faith and trust in God. God's last words to him portend a divine judgment—the Babylonian captivity (Isa. 39:1–7). This warning provides an apt setting for the background of the rest of the book of Isaiah, which consists of prophecies about the return from that captivity. In other words, the historical section (chs. 36–39) provides the proper context for reading the rest of the book, which is addressed to God's people in Babylon.

Speaking words of comfort to the exiles who are ready to return to the land (ch. 40), Isaiah recounts God's promise to prepare their way and bring them home. Humanity's feeble efforts to thwart God's promises are like grass that withers and falls when "the breath of the LORD blows on them" (Isa. 40:7). The Word of God, promised long beforehand and recorded by the prophet Isaiah (cf. 8:20; 30:8; 34:16), remains firm and "stands forever" (40:8). The coming of the Sovereign Lord to judge the nations and restore Jerusalem is now in sight, and no one can stand in his way: "Surely the nations are like a drop in a bucket" (40:15). God is the living God! He is incomparable, and no skilled craftsman can fashion an image of him. He is sovereign over all the nations and is the Creator of the universe. He gives strength to those who hope in him.

As the book nears its conclusion, a new character appears, the Servant of the Lord. Israel's salvation will be the work of this Servant (Isa. 52:13–53:12). He will offer himself as an atonement sacrifice for Israel and the nations. In his own day, no one will believe his message, though they will later turn to him and marvel at their former unbelief. This Servant, within the context of Isaiah, is the Davidic king (9:6), born as Immanuel (7:14), the Messiah. Within the context of the rest of the Bible, this Servant is Jesus.

Jeremiah

This book is by and about the prophet Jeremiah, who prophesies during the last days of the Israelite monarchy at the time of the Babylonian captivity (cf. Jer. 1:2). The main political power in his day is Babylon, led by the infamous Nebuchadnezzar. The last kings of Judah (Jehoiakim, Jehoiachin, and Zedekiah) are about to be defeated by Babylon, and Jerusalem will soon be destroyed.

In the face of this threat, Jeremiah proclaims that Babylon is the instrument of God's righteous wrath, who has been sent to punish the wicked nation of Judah. The only remedy is to submit to this punishment by submitting to the "yoke of Babylon." Those who oppose Jeremiah, on the other hand, object that God will never abandon his people, nor will he allow the house of David and the city of Jerusalem to be destroyed. Rather, as the false prophets proclaim, God will soon restore the fortunes of the house of David and Jerusalem, and they will return to their former glory (see Jer. 28:1–4).

In reply to the arguments of these false prophets, Jeremiah simply appeals to the terms of the Sinai covenant. Israel has sinned, he proclaims, and God, being a righteous God, will soon bring judgment against the sinful nation (cf. Deut. 27–29). However, like most of the prophets, Jeremiah also has a word of salvation. A time is coming when God will again bless his people. That time will be after the people's return from the Babylonian captivity—a captivity that will last seventy years (cf. Jer. 25:11–12; 29:10). The book of Jeremiah thus focuses the reader's attention on the events of the return from exile. At the close of the exile, Daniel himself wants to know if in his day Jeremiah's seventy years are completed (Dan. 9:1–2). God answers that the Messiah will not come in his day, for many more years must occur first (cf. 9:24–27).

There are many historical notes throughout the book, making sure that the reader views Jeremiah's message within the context of the exile to Babylon. In so doing, the book raises the question of whether the prophecies of Jeremiah—both the judgments and the anticipated blessings—are to be understood as fulfilled in the events of his own day, or whether they find their reference in events that lie in the future. For the most part, the New Testament writers see Jeremiah's prophecies as relating to the future, the time of the coming of Jesus Christ. This appears also to have been the viewpoint of the author of the book. An important part of his strategy in relating Jeremiah's words to historical events of his own day is to show that these events have come and gone; yet Jeremiah's words are still not fulfilled. Thus their fulfillment is to be related to an event yet in the future, namely, the coming of the Messiah.

Lamentations

This book begins by describing Jerusalem as it lies in ruins after the Babylonian destruction (Lam. 1:1–4). Like a forsaken widow, the city weeps bitterly in the night with no one to comfort her (vv. 1–2). There are no more appointed feasts (v. 4), all her gates are desolate (v. 4), her priests are groaning (v. 4), and she has become the slave of her enemies (v. 5). The author is quick to point out, however, the reason behind Jerusalem's misfortune: "The LORD has brought her grief because of her many sins" (v. 5). He gives full vent to the horrible notion that the Lord himself has become like Israel's enemy (ch. 2). That the Lord himself has brought on the destruction of Jerusalem understandably brings the author to the brink of despair (ch. 3).

At this point in the book, however, the writer remembers that all hope is not lost. There is still one last source of comfort—God's loyal love, his covenant faithfulness, his compassion that never ceases (Lam. 3:22). Out of the midst of the deepest despair of the exile springs new rays of hope: "Great is your faithfulness" (v. 23). With this hope comes a new call to life and faith in the Lord as well as a call to repentance (vv. 39–42). The basis of this hope is God's promise to send the Messiah through the house of David (2 Sam. 7).

In the last sections of the book a new note is sounded amid the voice of ruin. It is a call for God to recompense those who brought about this destruction (the Babylonians): "You have seen, O LORD, the wrong done to me. Uphold my cause!" (Lam. 3:59); "Pay them back what they deserve, O LORD, for what their hands have done" (v. 64); "Pursue them in anger and destroy them from under the heavens of the LORD" (v. 66). There is also a note of hope in the anticipation of a return from this exile: "O Daughter of Zion, your punishment will end; he will not prolong your exile" (4:22a).

In other words, Lamentations is a theological explanation of the Exile and destruction of Jerusalem. The Exile signaled that the days of Israel's reliance on the Lord's covenant, established with Israel at Sinai, were over. The covenant, or rather Israel's disobedience to the covenant, led to the Exile. But even though the Sinai covenant has been broken, Israel's relationship with the Lord is not over. The Lord will be faithful to his promises to David and the Davidic covenant (2 Sam. 7:16). There is thus hope. The faithful must trust in God's promises and wait patiently for the Lord's salvation (cf. Isa. 40:31). When Israel's punishment is complete, he will leave his people in exile no longer (Lam. 4:22; cf. Isa. 40:2). Thus restoration becomes the major theme on which the book concludes: "Restore us to yourself, O LORD, that we may return; renew our days as of old" (5:21).

Ezekiel

The book of Ezekiel is a first-person account of the prophet Ezekiel, who begins his prophetic ministry in the fifth year of Jehoiachin's exile to Babylon (592 B.C.). He is among the exiles and carries out his prophetic ministry in Babylon (Ezek. 1:1). He warns the people not to follow the words of the false prophets, who speak of the peace and blessing that is in store for them. Ruin, not peace, looms on their horizon. The people have rebelled against God and broken his covenant; consequently, they can only expect God's judgment. But Ezekiel also prophesies that peace and blessing will come to Israel in the future, after the time of judgment and destruction. Two major sections deal with these prophecies of hope: chapters 36–39 (the restoration of God's people) and 40–48 (the restoration of God's temple).

Ezekiel's group of visions contain mostly words of judgment against God's people who still remain in Judah and Jerusalem (Ezek. 1–24). These people will later be taken captive by the Babylonian king, Nebuchadnezzar. Interspersed among these words of doom and judgment are words of comfort and hope. Beginning in chapter 34, hope becomes the book's major focus.

Ezekiel also announces divine judgment against the other nations for their mistreatment of Israel (Ezek. 25–32). The basis of his oracles is God's promise to Abraham, "Whoever curses you I will curse" (Gen. 12:3). The nations enumerated in these chapters (identified as Israel's and God's enemies as early as the Pentateuch) will be destroyed because they rejoiced at the destruction of God's people. God's intent was to bless these nations through his own people, Israel, but Israel failed to obey God and followed instead in the ways of the other nations. Embedded in these oracles of judgment against the nations is a reminder of the hope that still lies ahead for the people of Israel (Ezek. 28:24–26).

Ezekiel's visions then turn to that of the restoration of the house of David (Ezek. 33–48). The fulfillment of his words of judgment on Jerusalem demonstrates the validity of his role as a prophet (33:33). That in turn serves as a basis for the reader's hope in the fulfillment of Ezekiel's words of blessing. Not only will the house of David be restored and Israel's enemies defeated, but the people of God will be returned to the land and be given a new heart (36:1–38). This is the new covenant, pictured here as a fulfillment of God's promise through Moses in Deuteronomy 30:4–6. Ezekiel's final vision is that of a new temple in Jerusalem (Ezek. 40:1–48:35). He gives much attention to detail, holding the grand picture of this temple before the eyes of the reader as long as possible—for most modern readers, too long! The restoration of the temple means the culmination of all God's promises of blessing and fellowship.

Daniel

The first chapter of Daniel introduces the book. It records the integrity of Daniel and his three friends as they refuse to eat the rich foods of the Babylonian king; as true Israelites, they remain faithful to God's covenant even in the most adverse circumstances.

Nebuchadnezzar's dream and Daniel's interpretation in chapter 2 provide the framework for most of the other events and visions that follow. In it God shows not only the whole panorama of the future of his and subsequent human kingdoms in this world but also the plan he has for his own chosen people. Chapters 3–6, which narrate four key episodes in the lives of the kings of Daniel's day, each have features that parallel aspects of Nebuchadnezzar's dream in chapter 2. The gold image the king sets up in his kingdom (ch. 3) reflects the image with the gold head of chapter 2. That kingdom, likened to a tree that grows until it is "visible to the ends of the earth" (4:11) but is reduced to ruin by God, contrasts with God's kingdom in chapter 2, which begins as a stone and becomes a mountain that fills the whole earth. Belshazzar's kingdom "is divided and given to the Medes and Persians" (5:28), like the "divided kingdom" of iron and clay in Nebuchadnezzar's dream. At the close of chapter 6, Darius proclaims that God "is the living God and he endures forever; his kingdom will not be destroyed" (6:26), using the exact words of Daniel's interpretation of Nebuchadnezzar's dream in 2:44.

The visions in Daniel 7 are not only central in importance to this book, but they also provide the basis for much of the messianic hope in the rest of the Bible. Their focal point is the appearance of the Son of Man in the clouds to receive the eternal kingdom from the Ancient of Days (Dan. 7:13–14). The imagery and ideas here are taken from 2 Samuel 7—the promise of an eternal kingship in Jerusalem that God made to the house of David.

Will the kingdom of these chapters be established at the return from Babylonian captivity, or will it come at a much later period? Daniel 9 answers this question by extending the seventy years of Jeremiah's prophecy by a multiple of seven. An anointed one, the Messiah, will come to establish an eternal kingdom after a time of seven and sixty-two weeks.

Daniel closes by directing his attention to a king distinct from all other kings (Dan. 11:36–45). This king will exalt himself against God and seek to overcome the other kingdoms and the Holy Land itself. He is to be identified with the final king, the Antichrist, known in the other visions as the "little horn" (ch. 7), the "strong king" (ch. 8), and the statue that falls from being struck by the falling rock (ch. 2). As an example for all believers, Daniel must carry on until the time of the end, when he will be resurrected with all who receive their eternal reward.

Hosea

This book describes God's relationship to Israel in terms of the prophet's own unfortunate marriage. Hosea's first marriage to a prostitute (Hos. 1:2–2:23) symbolizes Israel's and Judah's apostasy, while the faithfulness of Hosea to his wife symbolizes God's faithfulness to Israel. The Lord's love for Israel is characterized as "loyal love"—a steadfast love for his own chosen people. God is determined to remain faithful to the covenant regardless of Israel's unfaithfulness. He shows this loyal love to thousands of generations who obey and love him. In spite of all that happens to Israel, this love cannot be quenched (11:8–11).

But Israel has sinned and will be cast away from God's presence. This prophecy against them is based squarely on the stipulations of the Mosaic law, that the Lord is a jealous God and Israel is to have no other gods before him (Ex. 20:1–6). But Israel has been looking to other nations for help (Egypt and Assyria) rather than to the Lord; thus, they will go into exile in Assyria. This is seen as a return to the bondage of Egypt (Hos. 8:13; 9:3, 6; cf. 11:5). In this coming judgment on the northern kingdom, Judah will be delivered from Israel's fate. In the future, however, God will have compassion on Israel and regather them from among the nations and, with Judah, they will again dwell in the land. The exodus of God's people from Egypt as recounted in the Pentateuch becomes a picture of Israel's future salvation. That is, Israel's punishment is not permanent rejection, for the Lord will again bring his people back into the Promised Land and care for them as at the beginning (Hos. 2:16–25; 3:5; 11:8–11; 14:2–10).

Hosea's second marriage to a prostitute, with the intent of curing her of her prostitution, symbolizes God's use of the exile to cure Israel of apostasy (Hos. 3:1–5). The mention of David in 3:5 is derived from God's promise to David in 2 Samuel 7:16—the Messiah is to be a king of the house of David, and when he comes he will rule like David. Thus Hosea, who lived long after the time of David, can still look forward to a time when Israel "will return and seek the LORD their God and David their king" (3:5).

The past sins of Israel and Judah (Hos. 9:10–14:9) provide the context for viewing their present sin and for showing God's loyal love for Israel. The past is a parable (12:10). God has long endured his disobedient people, but his love for them remains. God will not forsake them forever (11:8–11). In keeping with the parabolic nature of this book, the author closes by calling for careful and discerning reading (14:9). A wise reader will gain much understanding from this book; a rebellious reader will stumble.

Joel

This book begins with a call to the wise (the elders) to seek understanding and pass it on to their children (Joel 1:2–3); this follows close on the heels of Hosea's admonition to the wise in Hosea 14:9. Throughout the book the reader is continually reminded of the impending "day of the LORD," a phrase that unifies the book (Joel 1:15; 2:1, 11, 31; 3:14).

The description of a devastating locust plague serves as a symbolic anticipation of the coming day of the Lord (Joel 1:15). All the normal divine provisions that Israel enjoyed will be removed in an instant, and the wise and discerning must prepare for the coming judgment. That day will soon come like an invasion that overtakes the land by surprise: "Like dawn spreading across the mountains a large and mighty army comes" (Joel 2:2b). The prophet's words reach epic proportions: "Before them fire devours, behind them a flame blazes" (2:3). His description assures the reader that the mighty hand of God lies behind this scene, for this is the army of God: "The LORD thunders at the head of his army" (2:11); this is the "day of the LORD" (2:11b).

The only way for Israel to avert the impending judgment of God is to repent and turn to him (cf. 2:13–15). There is hope for Israel, for God will restore their blessing. They need not fear or be sorrowful, for God has not forsaken his people. Instead, the "people of Zion" should rejoice and be glad (2:23), for "never again will my people be shamed" (2:26–27).

Thus the book calls the reader to a decision to repent. In other words, the addressees of the book go far beyond those of the original prophet, for his words address all generations of God's people as they await the coming of divine judgment upon the world. The basis of his call to repentance is the wonderful grace and compassion of God (Joel 2:13b). If the people repent, the Lord will "take pity on his people" (2:18) and drive the invading army far from them (2:20).

But before "the day of the LORD" comes, God will pour out his Spirit on all humanity. Salvation will come from Zion, the city of Jerusalem—this same emphasis on the work of the Spirit and Israel's obedience can be found in Ezekiel 36:24–27. God's work in the future will be marked by a new outpouring of his Spirit on all people. When blessing is restored to Israel, God will judge the nations who have oppressed them. Peter identifies the coming of the Spirit at Pentecost as the fulfillment of this prophecy (Acts 2:16).

Amos

The book is about the prophet Amos, a shepherd who was called by God to prophesy to the people of Israel, the northern kingdom (Amos 7:15). Amos apparently carries out most of his mission at the worship center at Bethel—a sanctuary of the king and palace (7:13). He preaches fearful words of impending doom against them, summarized by the priest Amaziah: "Jeroboam will die by the sword, and Israel will surely go into exile" (7:11).

Within the book itself, Amos stresses the moral ruin of God's people (Amos 2:6–8; 3:9–10; 5:7–12) and their mistaken presumption that since they are the elect, nothing ill can happen to them (3:2; 9:7). God's people mistakenly presume that as long as they keep up their external forms of worship, the Lord will not let them perish.

The book picks up the same theme on which the book of Joel ended: God's judgment against the nations. The irony of Amos' words, however, is that Israel and Judah are themselves included among those who will be judged. Because these two nations have strayed far from the covenant, they too will be treated like those outside the covenant. If God punishes the nations for their wickedness, how much more will he punish Israel and Judah! They should know better, given their special status before God.

Amid the visions of the book, the author places a narrative of his prophetic ministry (Amos 7:10–17), which provides an historical reference point for the prophecies that precede and follow it. His words refer to the sins of King Jeroboam and his false worship center at Bethel, as well as to the failure of the prophets to speak out against them. The prophets have so failed in their task that it is necessary for God to call a farmer, a layperson, to deliver his words. This narrative also shows that Amos is referring to the impending exile (7:17); thus, Israel's ultimate hope lies beyond the time of captivity that faces them in the immediate future (cf. Isa. 36–39).

The final vision in the book (Amos 9:1–15) contains not only a word of judgment but also a word of salvation. The judgment serves to put salvation into the perspective of God's wrath and mercy. Note that the word of salvation is based on God's promise to David in 2 Samuel 7 (the Davidic covenant). "David's fallen tent" (Amos 9:11) will rise up again at a time of future blessing and salvation. This refers to the restoration of the Davidic house and the coming of the messianic king. Though the house of David has been decimated by the exile, there is hope for the future because God made an eternal promise to the house of David.

Obadiah

Within the context of the Minor Prophets, the words of Obadiah against Edom (Obad. 1) pick up the lead of Joel 3:19 and Amos 1:11. The people of Edom represent the nations who are the enemies of God's people (the name "Edom" in Hebrew is virtually the same as the word for "nations"). The book of Obadiah portrays God's judgment on these nations. By contrast, the book of Jonah that follows portrays God's blessing and salvation of the nations. Thus, together, Obadiah and Jonah give the full picture of God's concern for the nations. He will judge the nations who turn against his people (Obadiah), but he will bless the nations who heed the words of his prophets (Jonah).

Obadiah falls naturally into two parts. The first section (Obad. 1–16) recounts the words of God's judgment against the nation of Edom for their mistreatment of the people of Judah. The complaint of the prophet is that the Edomites rejoiced to see destruction come on Jerusalem and Judah. They "stood aloof while strangers carried off [Israel's] wealth and foreigners entered [their] gates and cast lots for Jerusalem" (v. 11). They rejoiced when Judah was destroyed (v. 12) and "wait[ed] at the crossroads to cut down their fugitives" (v. 14).

The second section (Obad. 17–21) turns to the theme of salvation and deliverance for God's people—a common theme in the prophets: Salvation will come to Zion (v. 17a), and God's people will receive their due inheritance (v. 17b). On that day, the nation of Israel will turn the tables on Edom and conquer them (v. 18). This will fulfill of the prophecy of Balaam in Numbers 24:18, thus signaling the coming of the messianic age. In the logic of the imagery of this book, Israel's conquering Edom signifies that Edom, and thus all "nations," will become a part of God's kingdom. When the Deliverer(s) who rules on Mount Zion governs the mountains of Edom (v. 21a), it will mean that Edom has become a part of God's kingdom.

In these last verses of Obadiah, the prophet takes the image of the Deliverer(s) conquering Edom (Num. 24:18) and turns it into an image of Edom's seeking the Lord by becoming a part of God's kingdom. This is precisely the way the apostle James reads the nearby text of Amos 9:12. While the Hebrew text reads, "They [Israel] may possess the remnant of Edom," James paraphrases it, "the remnant of men may seek the Lord" (Acts 15:17). To be conquered by God's King is to become a part of God's kingdom.

Jonah

The book of Jonah is a narrative of one prophet's dealings with God and the nations. Its primary focus is on Jonah and reveals something important about the character of God, in that his mercy and salvation extend to all nations (Gen. 12:2–3). Jonah, the reluctant prophet, is slow to appreciate this feature of God's grace. He prefers to see God's grace and mercy limited to his own people.

The book opens with God's call to Jonah to preach against the wickedness of the city of Nineveh. This city represents the great kingdoms of this world that stand in opposition to God's people and his kingdom. Jonah disobeys God's call and sets out in the opposite direction, "headed for Tarshish" (Jonah 1:3)—somewhere in the direction of modern Spain. God's plan to reach Nineveh with his word of judgment is, however, not thwarted by Jonah's disobedience. He throws up obstacles into his way. First he hurls (1:4) a great storm into the sea where Jonah is fleeing, which results in Jonah himself being hurled (1:15) into the sea, where he is found by a great fish appointed by God "to swallow Jonah" (1:17). God is in control of his world, and Jonah cannot hide from him. His disobedience, in fact, becomes the very means whereby God's grace is extended to the Gentiles. When the sailors see God's calming of the sea on Jonah's behalf, they "greatly feared the LORD, and they offered a sacrifice to the LORD and made vows to him" (1:16). In other words, the men put their faith in God. Ironically Jonah's rejection of God's command has led to the salvation of the Gentiles.

The second scene of the book occurs in the belly of the great fish. There we overhear Jonah's rejoicing and praise to God at having been rescued. This psalm clearly shows that Jonah, and thus also the author of the book, sees the great fish as an instrument of God's salvation.

In Jonah 3, Jonah does not preach long before the people of Nineveh turn from their idols and put their trust in God. God has mercy on them when they repent and believe, and he rebukes his own (Jonah) for his hardness of heart. The book focuses on the reluctance of Jonah to acknowledge the universal scope of God's grace. Indeed, we are not even sure at the end of the book that Jonah himself gets the message, though the message is clear to the readers—God has compassion on all his creatures. Jonah's petty concern for the vine that shields him from the sun (4:6–8) is a picture of the reader's own self-pity and lack of concern for the nations. Thus, God's question at the close of the book, "Should I not be concerned about that great city?" (4:11), confronts each reader of the book.

Micah

The prophet Micah, a contemporary of Isaiah, begins by portraying the Lord as the judge of all the earth coming in judgment on his own people, Israel. The central problem he confronts is the sin of idolatry (Mic. 1:5ff.) and injustice (2:1ff.). As in Isaiah, the instrument of God's wrath is the nation of Assyria, though the identity of this nation is concealed in the first pronouncement of judgment (in 1:15, Assyria is called simply "a conqueror"; cf. 5:5). The punishment that awaits the sinful people is exile from the land (1:16; 2:3–5).

Abruptly the book turns from judgment to salvation—the return of the people from exile. Micah envisions a time when the people of Israel will return from captivity led by their king, the Lord their God (cf. Isa. 40:3ff.). Then, just as abruptly, he returns to the theme of judgment against the unjust and against the leaders of God's people who presume upon God's grace (Mic. 3:11). Again the punishment is exile (3:12), but it is followed by five pronouncements of salvation: salvation for the nations at Zion (4:1–5), salvation for the regathered remnant (4:6–7), salvation for the victorious remnant (4:8–13), salvation for the ruler of the remnant (5:1–5a), and salvation for the nations of the earth (5:5b–9).

The Promised Ruler in 5:1–5a will come from Bethlehem and will lead the victorious remnant in defeat of their enemy. The small will overcome the mighty "in the strength of the LORD" (Mic. 5:4). This is a messianic promise of central importance to the Bible. It alludes to the Immanuel prophecy in Isaiah 7:14 and to the birth of the Davidic king, who is called "Almighty God" in Isaiah 9:6.

Assyria's guilt is clearly described in Micah 5:10–15 and is summed up in the phrase, "upon the nations that have not obeyed me" (5:15b). Any nation (Assyria or Israel) that sins grievously (cf. 7:9) and does not obey God will be judged. By contrast, what pleases God is "to act justly and to love mercy and to walk humbly with your God" (6:8). One must wait for God's salvation in the future (7:7), when the enemy will be destroyed (7:10); at that time all the nations will enjoy God's salvation (7:12). That future salvation is as sure as Israel's salvation in the past because God is faithful to his promises (7:14–20).

The book closes with a reference to the Abrahamic covenant, God's promise to Abraham of a great nation and possession of the land (Gen. 12:1–9). The basis of Micah's hope is thus the message of the Pentateuch. God's promises are sure. He will fulfill them just as he has promised the fathers "in days long ago" (Mic. 7:20).

Nahum

The prophet Nahum prophesies in the southern kingdom of Judah during the last decades of the dynasty of David. He begins with a hymn depicting the glory of the Lord and proclaiming the Lord as a mighty and righteous God who rules not only among his own people but also over all of his universe (Nah. 1:1–14). Thus Nahum sees God's relationship to Israel both through the lens of the covenant and through the lens of creation. He proclaims comfort (note: the name *Nahum* means *comfort* in Hebrew) to Judah by noting that the Lord will judge their bitter enemy, the Assyrians. This mighty nation, which has by now overrun Judah and Israel for many years, has transgressed God's edict. Assyria now stands under the impending judgment of God and will quickly pass from the scene of world history (Nah. 1:15b).

Nahum draws out the implication of Nineveh's destruction for Judah. Simply put, it means Judah's salvation (Nah. 1:15; 2:2). There is always a note of salvation in the midst of the prophets' threats of judgment. The reader's attention is directed to the "one who brings good news, who proclaims peace" (1:15). The picture draws on the imagery and hope established elsewhere in the Old Testament (cf. Gen. 49:10; Isa. 9:6).

The destruction of Nineveh is portrayed in graphic detail. The point of this depiction is to emphasize that it is the Lord who has brought this against them: "'I am against you,' declares the LORD Almighty. 'I will burn up your chariots in smoke'" (Nah. 2:13). Moreover, the book intends to show that God has done this great deed in order to "restore the splendor of Jacob" (2:2). In other words, behind the events of history stands the sovereign power of God, and behind that power stands God's purpose. The nations have mistreated Israel, and God will not let that go unpunished. This is the lesson of God's covenant with Abraham. God had promised, "Whoever curses you I will curse" (Gen. 12:3).

The fall of Nineveh is recounted a second time in order to put it in context with God's ongoing work of judgment against the nations (Nah. 3:8–11). What God has done to Nineveh is merely an example of his actions among the other nations. No nation, not even the mighty Assyrian empire, can escape the chastening hand of God. Assyria scattered God's people, and now they themselves "are scattered on the mountains with no one to gather them" (3:18).

Habakkuk

This book opens with a short account of Habakkuk's lament (Hab. 1:1–4). Looking around him the prophet sees violence and distress on all sides. It is difficult to say precisely what he sees. Is it the sins of his own people? Or the terrible oppression of a foreign invasion? The author keeps Habakkuk's words as general as possible, thus making those words applicable to any situation. The prophet speaks for all the righteous who are distressed by the rampant disregard of God's law. His central concern is to know, "How long?" Will God tolerate such evil without ever sending judgment?

Habakkuk's lament is interrupted by a word from God. God says, in effect, "A work is being done that many will not believe when they hear of it" (Hab. 1:5). These words challenge even Habakkuk to look more closely at what he is lamenting to see if perhaps something of the work of God is already being accomplished in his midst. Just as in Habakkuk's lament, the "work" God speaks of here is not defined. In the immediate context it consists of God's sending a great and fearful nation against Habakkuk's own countrymen (1:6–11) as a work of judgment (1:12b). Later biblical writers identified this "work" with the coming of the Messiah and his sacrificial death on the cross (Acts 13:41). Since the author himself links the work of God in Habakkuk 1:5 with the messianic work of God in salvation (3:2), the New Testament interpretation of this passage appears to be right on the money.

Thus, the revelation that Habakkuk received from God "awaits an appointed time . . . and will not prove false" (Hab. 2:3). Evil men and mighty nations will come and go (2:5–19), but the Lord will see to it that they reap the wages of their wicked deeds (2:13, 16b). Furthermore, God has established a time when he will come in great glory and bring salvation to the faithful (3:3–15). When he hears this, Habakkuk cannot wait for God's timing. He calls on God to do it in his own day: "I stand in awe of your deeds, O Lord. Renew them in our day, in our time make them known" (3:2).

Though he calls for God's action now, Habakkuk is willing to "wait patiently" (Hab. 3:16b) because the Lord is his strength (3:19). In him is his joy (3:18). The final lesson of the book, then, is the admonition for the godly to wait patiently and faithfully on the Lord. God is already at work. The faithful can see his hand in the events around them. Their task is to wait for God's appointed time and to rejoice in his salvation.

Zephaniah

It is fitting that this book revolves around the theme of the day of the Lord—the same day that closed the book of Habakkuk. The prophet Zephaniah announces of the coming "day of the LORD." His opening chapter describes the impending "day" of judgment against "all who live in the earth" (Zeph. 1:18), though the focus of the pronouncement is that both Israel and Jerusalem stand under God's wrath (1:10–12). Thus the scope of the book is the whole of God's people. In God's plan there is a future for all the seed of Abraham (cf. Gen. 12:2–3).

This cosmic scope of the divine judgment is established by means of a series of allusions to the creation account in Genesis. Just as God filled the whole of his creation with animals, birds, fish, and humankind (Gen. 1), so also in judgment he will wipe out all of these creatures, including humanity (Zeph. 1:2–3). Just as the creation account in Genesis focuses on the land, so also here God's judgment focuses on the land (1:4–13). Judah stands under God's wrath because they have forsaken him and followed after gods of their own making (1:5, 9b), rather than worshiping the Lord, in whose image they were created (Gen. 1:26).

The description of the "day of the LORD" concludes with a brief call to the righteous to seek the Lord and find refuge in him from the wrath to come (Zeph. 2:3). The righteous are those who put their trust in God during those days of distress. They wait for the "appointed time" (cf. Dan. 12:4; Hab. 2:3) to come by seeking righteousness and humility (Zeph. 2:3b).

Zephaniah then brings the nations into the sphere of the day of the Lord. God's judgment extends beyond his people Israel. The nations that have historically oppressed Israel are selected and warned of the coming day of divine wrath: Philistia (Zeph. 2:4–7), Moab and Ammon (2:8–11); Cush (i.e., Egypt; 2:12), and Assyria (2:13–15). The prophet then turns to Jerusalem, who "does not trust in the LORD" (3:2). God's people have not learned from the experiences of the other nations, so they too will suffer God's judgment. A righteous God dwells within their midst (3:5), and they are as subject to his wrath as are the other nations (3:5b–7).

But the purpose of divine judgment is salvation. God wants to purify the nations "that all of them may call on [i.e., worship] the name of the LORD" (3:9). In that day, the nations will be purified of the proud and arrogant, and only the humble will remain along with the remnant of Israel (3:12–13). In other words, after judgment comes salvation. Israel's blessing will be restored and the exiles will be returned to Jerusalem (3:20). The focus of the message of salvation is the hope of the return from Babylonian captivity. As is true of most of the prophetic literature, the return from Babylon is used as an image of the future messianic age.

Haggai

The prophet Haggai preaches to those who have returned from Babylonian captivity and are living in Jerusalem (ca. 520 B.C.). His first oracle (Hag. 1:1–11) sets the tone: God's people have returned to Jerusalem, but the temple still lies desolate (1:9). Thus Israel remains under God's judgment (1:10–11). The faithful few (e.g., Zerubbabel and Joshua; 1:12–15) become a model for what has to be done to receive God's promised blessing.

In the second oracle (Hag. 2:1–9), the hope for the future is renewed. A temple even more glorious than Solomon's will be built from the wealth of the nations (2:6–9). This future rebuilding is now the focus of Israel's trust and confidence in God and his promises. The oracle is addressed to Zerubbabel, son of Shealtiel, who as the scion of the house of David is heir to the messianic promise (2 Sam. 7:14–16). The time is ripe for fulfillment.

The concern for building the temple in the messianic age can be seen in Haggai 2:6–7: "'In a little while I will once more shake the heavens and the earth, the sea and the dry land . . . and the desired of all nations will come, and I will fill this house with glory,' says the LORD Almighty." The event the prophet has in view is clearly the future messianic kingdom. But who or what is the "desired of all nations?" Some take this to mean simply the gold and precious materials gathered from the nations that will be used to build the temple. It is more likely, however, that this refers to the Messiah himself, the one who is desired by all nations. When the temple is built, that will signal his coming.

The third oracle (Hag. 2:10–19) provides the important interpretive clue to the relationship of the present temple to the future one. The present temple cannot be the future one because the present remnant (those who have returned to the land of Israel in Haggai's day) is not yet like the expected future remnant. They are unclean, and so is the work of their hands, the present temple (2:14). Thus, the long-awaited blessing was still to come (2:19), though the present temple is a visible sign that the future temple will surely be built (2:15, 18).

In the fourth oracle (2:20–23) the present leader (Zerubbabel) becomes a sign of the future leader (the Messiah). The historical return from Babylonian captivity and the rebuilding of the temple by Zerubbabel is not the fulfillment of the hope of the prophets. But the response of the people to the words of the prophet and their willingness to begin work on the temple serve as a model of the faithful remnant of the future. That remnant will one day follow the Messiah and rebuild the temple in Jerusalem, thus fulfilling all the promises of the prophets.

Zechariah

The book of Zechariah shows that the fulfillment of the messianic promises to David (2 Sam. 7) will come only when Israel completely obeys God's will. In other words, the fulfillment is conditional: "This will happen if you diligently obey the LORD your God" (Zech. 6:15; cf. 3:7 ; 7:9–14; 8:14–17; also Ezek. 36:24–28). Since Israel and Jerusalem in Zechariah's own day do not come close to meeting that standard, Zechariah demonstrates that the coming of the Messiah and the promised "return" from captivity is something yet to happen.

Zechariah makes his case first by means of eight symbolic night visions, which show that the seventy years of captivity are nearly complete and the temple is about to be rebuilt (Zech. 1:7–17). Israel's enemies will be destroyed (1:18–21), and Jerusalem will be rebuilt as a habitation for all nations (2:1–13). Israel must obey God to enjoy the promised blessing (3:1–10). The work of God in establishing his kingdom will be by the power of his Spirit (4:1–14). Justice will be administered throughout the entire land (5:1–4); wickedness will be removed and taken to Babylon (5:5–11); God's wrath will be meted out against the land of the north (6:1–8). Joshua the high priest is symbolic of the "priest-king" Messiah (cf. Ps. 110), who is yet to come.

In the messianic age, God will again dwell in Jerusalem. It will again be called "the City of Truth" (Zech. 8:3) and will be a place of joy and salvation (8:4–8), peace (8:9–11), prosperity (8:12), and blessing (8:13). Worship of God will be restored to Zion, and peoples from all nations and tribes will come to Jerusalem to worship him (8:20–23). As a prelude to the coming of the messianic King, God will purge the nations so that they too will become his people.

The focal point of Zechariah's vision of salvation for Israel is the Promised King, who will rule the nations in peace and righteousness (Zech. 9:9–10; cf. Pss. 2; 72). He will be the good shepherd. But the people will not want to be ruled by him. They will rebel and dismiss him for "thirty pieces of silver" (Zech. 11:12)—a picture that finds its fulfillment in the coming of Christ and his rejection. A worthless shepherd will then lead them to slaughter as part of God's judgment against his disobedient people. But a day is coming when God will restore the peace of Jerusalem. A great battle will precede this time of peace. Jerusalem will be surrounded by many nations, but God will deliver his city and his people.

Malachi

The prophet Malachi carries out his prophetic work during the days after the return from the Babylonian captivity. The name of Malachi (meaning "my messenger") symbolically anticipates the prophecy regarding God's final "messenger" announced in Malachi 3:1 and the prophecy of the return of Elijah in 4:5. That future prophet will be much like the present Malachi, in that he will prepare the nation for the coming of God's kingdom. The "messenger" (a word that can also be translated "angel") in Malachi continues the thought of Zechariah, who briefly focused on the "Angel of the LORD" who went before the people of God to prepare the way of salvation (Zech. 12:8).

This book, which contains words of warning to the present sinful nation, is a model of the warning to be announced by God's coming messenger. When that messenger comes, he will carry out a role similar to that of Malachi. The book itself is arranged around a series of six disputes between Malachi and the people, in which the prophet builds a case against them, demonstrating that they are not yet ready for the coming of the Promised King. (1) God has cared for Israel throughout all the past, but the people do not recognize or appreciate God's care (Mal. 1:2–5). (2) The people treat their offerings carelessly and thus dishonor God (1:6–2:9). (3) Israel is profaning the covenant by marrying pagan women (2:10–16). (4) Though Israel may think God will never carry out his plan of judgment against unrighteousness, he will soon send his messenger to do so (2:17–3:5). (5) Israel is withholding their tithes, but if the people give to God, he will more abundantly bless their land (3:6–12). (6) Though Israel is tired of waiting for God's blessing, those who wait on the Lord and fear him will have a portion in the coming divine blessing (3:13–18). Waiting on the Lord consists in obediently trusting God to fulfill his promises and to send his future prophet to prepare the people for the coming of God's kingdom.

In the Hebrew Bible, the last verses of Malachi serve as a link between the major segments of the canon—that is, the Prophets and the Writings. As such they parallel the canonical links between the Pentateuch (Torah) and the Prophets (Deut. 34 and Josh. 1). Both Malachi 4 and Deuteronomy 34 look forward to the coming of a prophet who will usher in the messianic age. Both Joshua 1 and Psalm 1 focus the reader's attention on the written word of God. Thus in the shape of the Hebrew Bible, there is an anticipation of the coming messianic age that the prophets have announced; at the same time, these canonical links stress the importance of Scripture as a guide to living until that age arrives.

The New Testament

Matthew

The Gospel of Matthew begins with the genealogy of Jesus (Matt. 1:1–17), tracing his lineage back through David to Abraham. Jesus was the son of David, a legitimate heir to the title of Messiah, and a descendant of Abraham, a legitimate heir to the blessing of Abraham. This Gospel has a clear structure, alternating between narratives of the life of Jesus and discourses that give account of his teaching. Each discourse section closes with a similar formula: "When Jesus had finished saying these things ..." (7:28; 11:1; 13:53; 19:9; 26:1).

After recording the infancy of Jesus, showing how he fulfills various Old Testament prophecies (Matt. 1:18–2:23), the author gives three events out of the period of preparation for Jesus' ministry: (1) the ministry of John the Baptist (3:1–12); (2) Jesus's baptism in the Jordan (3:13–17); and (3) the temptation of Jesus (4:1–11). In this way Matthew affirms Jesus' identity as the true Messiah, the Son of God. Thereupon he recounts, in summary form, the message of Jesus in his Sermon on the Mount (chs. 5–7).

To illustrate the authority of Jesus, Matthew records several incidents that focus on the recognition of his authority among the people and the Jewish leaders (Matt. 8:1–9:38). These correspond to the list of evidences given to the imprisoned John the Baptist (11:2–6).

Jesus sent his disciples throughout the land of Israel to announce the coming of the messianic king (Matt. 10). This served as the prelude to the leader's rejection of the king in chapter 12 and their plot to crucify Jesus. He is identified as the Servant of the Lord "in [whose] name the nations will put their hope" (12:21).

The kingdom Jesus offers is illustrated in seven parables. He came to establish the kingdom promised in the Old Testament prophetic literature. That kingdom, however, which will be a visible, universal rule of the Messiah, begins in a small, almost imperceptible form—as a mustard seed or a piece of yeast in a lump of dough. Members of the kingdom must live in expectation of the return of the King at the "end of the age."

Matthew continues with a selection of the works of Jesus along an itinerary through Galilee (Matt. 14:1–16:12), by means of which he authenticates Jesus' words. Before the account of Jesus' crucifixion in Jerusalem, our Lord spoke of the establishment of his church (chs. 16–20), which would be based on the work he was about to accomplish. He had to "suffer many things ... [and] be killed and on the third day be raised to life" (16:21).

On arriving in Jerusalem, the crowds looked to Jesus as their Messiah. But the tables quickly turned (Matt. 21–22). This became the occasion for his last discourse to the crowds (ch. 23) and to his disciples on the Mount of Olives (chs. 24–25). Jesus voluntarily gave up his life (chs. 26–27). But Matthew ends on a note of hope, Jesus' resurrection. Having met his disciples in Galilee, he sent them out, promising to be with them until the end of the age (28:19).

Mark

The meaning of the Gospel of Mark can be seen most clearly in the content as well as the overall structure or shape that the author gives to the book. He does not include many of the aspects of Jesus' ministry found in the other Gospels. There is no discussion of his birth, early life, family, and genealogy. Rather, he begins briefly with the ministry of John the Baptist, who announced the coming of the eschatological Messiah (Mark 1:2–8). Moreover, there is little about Jesus' teaching, for Mark focuses on his actions and events. An important exception to this is the eschatological discourse of chapter 13, which betrays Mark's interest in the "last days" and Jesus' role in fulfilling the hope of ancient Israel.

Mark's primary interest lies in the key events of the last week in the ministry of Jesus Christ, namely, in his death and resurrection. Geographically and chronologically, the proportionally large final section of the book (Mark 11–16) is devoted solely to Christ's final seven days in Jerusalem. The major turning point in this Gospel comes with Peter's confession, "You are the Christ" (8:29), after which the author focuses on Jesus' coming death and resurrection: "He then began to teach them that the Son of Man must suffer many things and be rejected . . . and that he must be killed and after three days rise again" (8:31).

Throughout the book, the author strategically focuses the reader's attention on key, theologically important, aspects of Christ's ministry by means of summary statements and repetition. For example, the Gospel begins with the statement that Jesus is the "Christ, the Son of God" (Mark 1:1). At the close of the first section, the account of the ministry of John the Baptist, Jesus is confirmed as the messianic Son of God by a voice from heaven, "You are my Son, whom I love; with you I am well pleased" (1:11). At the very center of the book, on the Mount of Transfiguration, a voice from heaven again states, "This is my Son. . . . Listen to him!" (9:7). And at the end of the book the Roman centurion states, "Surely this man was the Son of God" (15:39).

Thus Mark's Gospel is concerned with the question of the identity of Jesus as the messianic Son of God. This picture of Jesus is consciously modeled on that of the Messiah in the Old Testament—the one who would come to deliver his own people but whom they would reject and scorn: "He was despised and rejected by men, a man of sorrows, and familiar with suffering. . . . He was despised, and we esteemed him not" (Isa. 53:3).

Luke

Luke begins with John the Baptist, the first key figure in the series of events in the unfolding of the message of this Gospel. John was the forerunner of the Messiah, not the Messiah himself. At his baptism, Jesus was declared to be the Son of God by a voice from heaven. The genealogy of Jesus, traced through Mary, confirms that he had no earthly father, but was "the son of God" (Luke 3:38; cf. 1:35). Jesus was then led by the Spirit into Galilee. Luke devotes much attention to his ministry there (chs. 4–9). Jesus did many miracles, which attracted much attention. Collectively they authenticated his claim to be the messianic Son of David.

Midway through the book, Jesus resolutely began his last journey to Jerusalem (Luke 9:51). His purpose was clear: "The Son of Man is going to be betrayed into the hands of men" (9:44), and he "must suffer many things and be rejected ... killed and ... raised to life" (9:22). Jesus arrived in Jerusalem ten chapters later. Much in these intervening chapters recount his teaching to his disciples and his deeds. His teaching focused the nearness of the kingdom of God (10:9) and the need to prepare for its coming. Representatives of God's kingdom are to be like lambs amid wolves (10:3). They must not seek personal gain, but must rely on the Lord's provision and accept the help and support of those who serve him (10:4–16).

With the ever-growing crowd pressing in on him, Jesus began to warn his disciples about the importance of sincerity and honesty before God (Luke 12:1–12). Greed and possessions can keep one from the kingdom of God (12:13–21). Trust in God, not wealth (12:22–34). Live in constant expectation of the coming Son of Man (12:35–40). The kingdom is not for the proud, but for the humble (14:7–11); not for the rich and exclusive, but for the poor, the crippled, the lame, and the blind (14:12–14).

Jesus entered Jerusalem, but his kingdom was rejected. Only his disciples recognized him as "the king who comes in the name of the Lord" (Luke 19:38); to the rest "it [was] hidden" (19:42). Jesus wept, knowing what great blessings Israel could have had and what great judgment lay ahead. As he taught in the temple, events turned quickly and decisively against him.

During the last Passover meal, Jesus spoke of his impending death and his future return to establish his kingdom. His death meant the sacrifice of his own body for his disciples and for all who would become his disciples (Luke 22:19), and the shedding of his blood was the beginning of the "new covenant" (22:20). He explained his death in terms of the "servant" prophecy of Isaiah 53, which "must be fulfilled" in him (Luke 22:37). In the trial, Pilate declared Jesus innocent (23:10–25), but the crowd wanted him crucified

(22:18–23). In the end, the governor gave in to their wishes (23:24–25), and Jesus was crucified. After his resurrection, it was not until Jesus explained the Old Testament Scriptures to the disciples and broke bread with them that "their eyes were opened and they recognized him" as the risen Lord (24:31).

John

John's intention in writing this Gospel is clear: "that you may believe that Jesus is the Christ, the Son of God, and that by believing you may have life in his name" (John 20:31). To "believe" is to have eternal life (3:16). John presents Jesus as the Word, who was with God before the creation of the world and by whom all things were created. Jesus, the Word made flesh, revealed God's grace and truth by living among his people. In him they saw God's glory.

John the Baptist introduced Jesus as the Old Testament Passover Lamb, a sacrifice to "take away the sin of the world" (John 1:29). Through John's identification of Jesus, the central message of this Gospel is established: Jesus is the Messiah foretold in the Old Testament. He came to Israel and was rejected; but in his rejection, other nations and people are now receiving him; thus God has offered his Passover Lamb for the sins of the whole world.

The author moves quickly to identify those among God's people Israel who did receive the light, beginning with the first disciples (John 1:35–51). When they heard John the Baptist identify Jesus, they turned and followed him (1:36–37). The simplicity of that first call is no doubt intended to illustrate what Jesus later taught: "My sheep listen to my voice; I know them, and they follow me" (10:27). Then the author recounts the signs Jesus performed among the Israelites, who ultimately rejected him (chs. 2–3), and among the Samaritans, who received him (ch. 4). Jesus did many other signs that authenticated his identity as the Son of God (chs. 5–6). At the Pool of Bethesda he healed a man who had been crippled thirty-eight years, the amount of time Israel wandered in the wilderness after their unbelief. He fed five thousand people and walked on the sea—two miracles closely resembling Moses' feeding Israel in the desert and his bringing them through the Red Sea. Jesus is thus presented as a new Moses, forming a new people of God.

John gives an extended summary of the various discourses of Jesus at the temple (John 7–8). There was a wide range of responses among the people and the Jewish leaders to the claims of Jesus. Repeatedly he stressed that his message came from God and that he himself had come from God. The opinions about him remained divided. The teachers of the law attempted to trap Jesus in matters of legal interpretation. Their blindness to the identity of Jesus is illustrated in the account of the healing of the blind man (chs. 9–10) and the raising of Lazarus (ch. 11) and was foretold expressly in the words of the prophet Isaiah (12:37–41).

In his farewell discourse to his disciples, Jesus began by stressing the importance of humility and love (John 13). Then, in the rest of his discourse (chs. 14–16) and in his prayer (ch. 17), he looked to the broad specter of the subsequent history of the church, in which the Holy Spirit would minister in his place. As the Son of God, he had come to fulfill the command of his Father to redeem his chosen people. As the Son of Man he had come to establish God's kingdom. That necessitated the cross (chs. 18–19) and the resurrection (ch. 20).

Acts

The book of Acts is a continuation of Luke's Gospel. It traces the course of events that carried the fledgling young church from Jerusalem to Rome. The author wanted to explain the Jews' rejection of Christ and the establishment of the Christian church.

Acts opens with Jesus teaching his disciples about the kingdom of God. Luke uses Peter's Pentecost sermon (Acts 2) to show that the messianic kingdom of David had been offered to Israel, but was rejected. The fate of the nation was sealed by their leaders' final rejection of Jesus (ch. 4). Only a remnant from the house of Israel followed Jesus (ch. 5).

The early church quickly spread through persecution and the ministry of its leaders: Stephen (Acts 6–8), Philip (ch. 8), Paul (ch. 9; 13ff.), and Peter (chs. 9–11). Luke records the details of two of Peter's miracles—the healing of the paralytic Aeneas (9:32–35), and the raising of Dorcas (9:36–43)—thus showing the apostolic credentials of Peter as he initiated a major transition in the nature of the early church as it moved from a predominately Jewish church to a predominately Gentile one. In the account of the conversion of Cornelius in Caesarea (10:1–11:18), the narrative shows that the church was not only open to Gentiles, but also that the stringent requirements of the Mosaic law had been lifted from them.

Two further events show the initial spread of the gospel: the establishment of the congregation in Antioch (Acts 11:19–30) and the persecution of the early Christian community by Agrippa (12:1–25). From that point on, the gospel began to spread to the ends of the earth through the missionary journeys of Paul. In three such journeys he evangelized the regions of Asia Minor and Greece. Paul and those with him "proclaimed the word of God" in the Jewish synagogues, but they were nearly always forced to go outside the limits of Judaism to gain a hearing. The result was that both Jews and Gentiles came to faith in Jesus as the Messiah.

The conversion of so many Gentiles raised a major problem for the early church and led to the first church council in Jerusalem, which faced the question: Must the new Gentile converts conform to the requirements of the Mosaic law? The Church's answer was, "No! The Gentiles who have come to faith in Jesus do not have to fulfill the law of Moses."

Paul not only continued to face controversy with fellow Christians, he was also falsely accused by the Jews of teaching against Israel and the law. He was arrested and sent to Caesarea and then Rome for trial and imprisonment. In recording the defense of his ministry before Christian and Jewish leaders, Acts repeatedly provides detailed exposition of the fundamental nature of Christian doctrine. The basis of the gospel is God's exaltation of Jesus in the resurrection, and through that resurrection God fulfilled his promises to David to establish an eternal kingdom.

Romans

Like the other works of the apostle Paul, the book of Romans is formally a letter. It is written to a specific church (Rome), has an introductory greeting (Rom. 1:1–7), and ends with a list of personal notes (16:1–27). This is where the similarity to a letter ends, however, since for the most part the book is an extended treatise on the nature of the gospel, with sustained argumentation throughout. Paul reasons, argues, gives examples, and exhorts his readers—all with the intent of making them strong in the faith.

Paul's central line of thought is justification by faith. Everyone has fallen short of God's righteousness, and all human efforts are futile. Judaism's reliance on the law of the Sinai covenant does not result in a right standing before God. The good news is that God, in his great grace, has sent his own Son, Jesus Christ, as a sin offering for humanity; through faith in him all are made righteous. There is no other way to obtain righteousness before God than by accepting God's gift in Christ. Only through Jesus can humanity find peace with God.

The central section of Paul's argument is stated clearly in Romans 3:21–26: the righteousness that makes one acceptable before God is available to all who believe. His argument is not simply "justification by faith," but also the denial of its opposite, "justification by works." Pride has no place in a system of faith-righteousness. Paul illustrates his point with the life of Abraham (ch. 4), Adam (ch. 5), Christ (ch. 6), himself (ch. 7), and all believers (ch. 8).

Having built a case for the gospel in the first eight chapters, Paul turns to two major questions. The first is God's continued faithfulness to the people of Israel. How does the gospel affect Israel's covenant promises? In Romans 9–11, Paul answers that God still intends to keep his covenant promises to Israel. At some future day they will turn to Christ in faith, and "all Israel" will be saved (11:12–32). Until then, the Gentiles have been grafted into the blessings of God and enjoy the privileges of being sons of God that rightfully belongs to Israel.

The second question is how the gospel affects the everyday life of the church (Rom. 12–15). The righteousness imparted freely to the believer must be worked out in every aspect of his or her life. The danger Paul anticipates in the church at Rome is a growing polarity within the body of Christ—some members usurping more than their share in the work and others doing less. The guiding principle is a mutual love for one another and a mutual concern for the spiritual growth of the church. Each member has been given a specific sphere where one's faith is exercised. Whatever your gift, he argues, use it as the exercise of the faith given you by God.

1 Corinthians

The argument of 1 Corinthians is closely tied to its occasion. Reports Paul has received about divisions and quarreling within the church at Corinth necessitate his addressing specific problems and questions decisively and with apostolic authority.

The theme Paul returns to throughout the book is that of the unity of the church, the body of Christ, and the importance of each member's concern and care for the others. All things must be done for the sake of building up the body of Christ. For Paul, this means the Christian life finds its reward in the blessing that awaits God's people at the return of Christ (1 Cor. 15), and work done for the Lord is never in vain (15:58). The hope of the resurrection thus lies behind most, if not all, of Paul's discussion.

Paul turns quickly to specific problems. The first of these is the quarrels and divisions among the members of the church (1 Cor. 1:10–4:21). Their leaders were apparently arrogantly asserting their own learned views on the nature and implications of Paul's gospel. Paul's response is complex, but underlying his remarks is his conviction that the message of the gospel is simple and can be understood in the ordinary language of common people.

Paul then turns to the question of sexual immorality within the Corinthian church (1 Cor. 5–6) and marriage (ch. 7). For their own good, Paul argues, sexual offenders should be put out of the church where, presumably, they will learn their lesson and repent. Regarding marriage, Paul asserts that it is good, but not the highest good. The highest good is serving the Lord.

So far, Paul has discussed black and white issues. What about gray areas, such as eating meat offered to idols? Here the principle of the weaker believer holds. Christians should respect the consciences of other believers. Though all things are permissible, the loving Christian always asks how one's actions will be understood by and affect a fellow believer. Will it cause them to stumble?

Paul then moves on to the conduct of the local church. Should women cover their heads when they pray in church? Yes, says Paul, this is an important symbol in worship. The manner in which the church celebrates communion is another important symbol; the purpose of that meal is not to satisfy hunger but to remember the work of Christ.

In Romans 12 Paul had argued that God gives spiritual gifts to members of the church. In 1 Corinthians 12–14, he stresses that the purpose of those gifts is the unity of the church and its growth in maturity. The church is like a body, with each part having a specific function. Spiritual gifts are that way. They should all work for the well-being of the whole. At the heart of the matter with spiritual gifts is that they should be exercised with love (ch. 13).

2 Corinthians

Second Corinthians is a letter; yet more than that, it is a monologue, with Paul delivering a barrage of words to his readers in Corinth, sometimes lamenting their misunderstanding of his motives, sometimes castigating those who are stirring up strife, and sometimes praising God for the blessings that came through his afflictions. With an unrelenting war of words, Paul raises and masterfully handles some of the most thorny issues of the gospel in the New Testament.

Paul begins by reminding them of the great suffering he has endured for the sake of the Christians at Corinth. He then reflects on the urgent need of a member of the church who had been severely disciplined. He should be restored, "so that he will not be overwhelmed by excessive sorrow" (2 Cor. 2:7). Paul's own ministry was based on the biblical principle of reconciliation. That in turn was based on the new covenant, by which the external law of God formerly written on tablets of stone has been replaced by the law of God written on human hearts (Jer. 31:33). The old covenant, with its passing glory, has seen its day. When a Christian renounces "secret and shameful ways" (2 Cor. 4:2a), does not use deception (4:2b), does not distort God's Word (4:2c), and lives a life with a clear conscience in the sight of God (4:2d), the glory of the new covenant shines "out of the darkness" (4:6). Such glory does not radiate from within Christians, however, for that treasure is located "in jars of clay" (4:7). This truth of the gospel keeps Paul from losing heart when he looks at what is happening to him. It also gives him hope for the eternal dwelling that awaits him when his temporary clay jar passes away (5:1–5).

Some people, Paul warns, who "take pride in what is seen rather than in what is in the heart" (2 Cor. 5:12), are turning the church against his apostolic leadership. They are not attacking Paul's authority as much as distorting the gospel he preaches. Thus, with the love of Christ and the truth of the gospel, Paul asserts his authority. That gospel is one of "God ... reconciling the world to himself in Christ, not counting men's sins against them" (5:19). It is the gospel of grace, which should be keep clear at all times (6:3–13) and never be linked with unbelief (6:14–18). It demands purity of life (7:1) and open acceptance of one another (7:2–4).

A major source of trouble for the church at Corinth was the presence of false apostles. Paul thus enters into a passionate defense of his apostolic ministry. He fears that someone may present the church with a "Jesus other than the Jesus [Paul] preached" (2 Cor. 11:4) and that the minds of believers "may somehow be led astray from [their] sincere and pure devotion to Christ" (11:3). Paul is determined not to adopt the methods of these "super-apostles," though he is not going to let them outboast him in matters that clearly demonstrate the sincerity of his ministry. Lest anyone mistake his motives, Paul reminds his readers that his boasting has been entirely limited "to things that show [his] weakness" (11:30–12:10).

Galatians

Some teachers in the churches of Galatia were persuading the Gentile Christians to seek to be justified before God by the requirements of the Mosaic law. For Paul, this represents "a different gospel" (Gal. 1:6), a distortion of the message he preached. After all, one "is not justified by observing the law, but by faith in Jesus Christ" (2:16). Ultimately, it is a question of Christ's work on the cross: "I have been crucified with Christ. . . . If righteousness could be gained through the law, Christ died for nothing!" (2:20–21).

But what about living the Christian life? Does that entail keeping the law? Having begun by faith, should one now turn back to the law? Is it the Spirit or human effort that empowers a Christian's life? According to Paul, the Old Testament Scriptures themselves taught that the Gentiles, apart from the law, would receive the gift of righteousness through faith alone.

What is life like under the law? "Cursed is everyone who does not continue to do everything written in the Book of the Law" (Gal. 3:10; cf. Deut. 27:26). That is, no one is righteous before God by the law, for "the law is not based on faith" (Gal. 3:12). Rather, "the man who does these things will live by them" (3:12). Thus, Gentiles can be given Abraham's blessing only by faith, and only by faith do we receive the promise of the Spirit (3:14).

The law did have a definite purpose, related to Israel's need for guidelines and help in their weakness, because of their numerous transgressions in the desert, especially that of the Golden Calf (Ex. 32). It was not given in order to impart life to them; rather, it held them, as it were, prisoners until the time when "faith should be revealed" (Gal. 3:23). But now that faith has come in Christ, Paul says, "we are no longer under the supervision of the law" (3:25).

Thus in Christ, all have become children of God. No longer are there to be distinctions such as Jews and Gentiles, slave and free, male and female. In Christ all are equally Abraham's descendants. In the divine plan of the ages, God sent Jesus to redeem his people from the law and to give them their full rights as his children. The Gentiles before the coming of Christ were enslaved to false gods in ignorance (Gal. 4:8). Now that Christ has come to set us free, why does anyone want to go back to this former state of slavery (4:9–20)?

The fact that Christians are not under the Mosaic law, however, does not mean they are free to live as they please. There is a higher law, "the law of Christ" (Gal. 6:2): "Love your neighbor as yourself" (5:14). If one lives by the Spirit, he or she will not "gratify the desires of the sinful nature" (5:16) but will exhibit the "fruit of the Spirit" (5:22–23), such as love, kindness, and self-control. These do not relate to mere external acts, but are matters of the heart.

Ephesians

Paul begins this letter with a panoramic view of God's plan for humankind, starting from eternity. Beginning with the divine blessings "in the heavenly realms" (Eph. 1:3), he views the Christian's life in Christ as one that draws on a treasure stored in heaven under God's safe-keeping. Before God created the world, he determined a plan for redeeming humanity. That plan involved the death of his Son, Jesus. As each individual Christian turns to Christ in faith, he or she is included in God's plan and is marked with the seal of the Holy Spirit (1:13–14).

Christians need enlightened hearts to know "the riches of [their] glorious inheritance" (Eph. 1:18). In Jesus' resurrection, God exalted Christ to his right hand and gave him dominion over all things. Gentiles were formerly "dead in [their] transgressions and sins," but so were Jews (2:1–3). Both were "objects of [divine] wrath" and in need of God's grace. But when God raised Jesus from the dead, he made believers "alive in Christ." All this by grace, in order to demonstrate "the incomparable riches of his grace" (2:7).

Earlier generations of God's people did not understand God's plan for the Gentiles as Paul now does. They were unaware that Jews and Gentiles would some day be united into one people in Christ (Eph. 3:6). Now, however, this mystery has been distinctly revealed. Paul himself was specifically called to make it clear. The riches stored up for believers is spiritual power for living a Christian life (3:16).

How is Christ's power to be lived out in everyday life? The main goal of each believer is to exhibit the love of Christ with one another. This is accomplished *in the church* by means of the gifts each member of the body has received and through achieving maturity in the knowledge of the truth (Eph. 4:1–16). An understanding of what God has done in Christ should also lead to a *transformed personal life*. Former ways of thinking must be consciously put aside and replaced with "true righteousness and holiness" (4:24). This includes speaking the truth; controlling anger; refusing to steal; doing hard work; sharing with others; talking cleanly; honoring the Spirit; ridding oneself of bitterness, rage, anger, brawling, and slander; being kind; and forgiving each other (4:25–32). Wives must submit to their husbands as they submit to Christ, and husbands must love their wives as Christ loved the church (5:22–33). Children must obey their parents, and parents are to be kind to their children (6:1–4). Servants must obey their masters sincerely, and masters will be held accountable before the Lord for how they treat their servants (6:5–9). Spiritual warfare exists in a Christian's life (6:10–18), and the kind of equipment needed for daily struggles with the old way of life is what the Spirit gives to the church.

Philippians

Paul wrote this letter to the church in Philippi out of a concern that the believers there should not veer away from the sincerity of their faith. He stresses that they have done well in the faith up to this point. But as in his own ministry, the greatest tests lie ahead. The key to the direction they should take is the example of Christ.

Apparently one of the problems in the Philippian church was a menacing factionalism, for which reason Paul cites several examples of humility. (1) Jesus himself lived a life of humility, "doing nothing out of selfish ambition or vain conceit" (Phil. 2:3). "Being in very nature God," he did not hesitate to "[make] himself nothing, taking the very nature of a servant" (2:6–7). Through such deep humility "God exalted him to the highest place" (2:9). (2) Timothy and Epaphroditus embody the kind of humility and love for the church that Paul wants the Philippians to have (2:19–30). (3) Paul then writes about himself as an example of humility (3:1- 21). (4) He concludes his survey with their own past acts of faithfulness (4:10–20).

In his warning against the false teachers among them—those threatening to turn the church in the wrong direction—we can see the reason for Paul's focus on humility. These would-be leaders stress "confidence in the flesh" (Phil. 3:3), elevating the importance of personal achievement and status over dependence on the work of Christ. Paul's argument against such claims stems from his own personal experience. Although he has more to boast than any of them in matters relating to personal achievement, he considers it all as "loss for the sake of Christ" (3:7). Paul wants only a righteousness "that comes from God and is by faith" (3:9).

Paul's ultimate goal is to "know Christ and the power of his resurrection" (Phil. 3:10). He admits he has not yet obtained this goal, but will continue to strive for it in the days ahead. This attitude is the mark of Christian maturity. Rather than follow those "enemies of the cross of Christ" who want earthly things and stress personal achievement and self-gratification (Phil. 3:18–19), Paul exhorts his readers to follow his example and to seek such people as their leaders.

Paul then addresses a problem of dissension between two faithful Christian women, Euodia and Syntyche (Phil. 4:1–3). He then broadens his appeal in general terms: rejoice, be gentle, do not be anxious, give thanks in everything, and think on what is true, noble, lovely, admirable, excellent, and praiseworthy (4:4–9). He closes the letter by thanking them for a gift they had sent him to help him in his ministry.

Colossians

Paul's primary concern for the church at Colosse is the threat of false teachers, with their man-made philosophies and religions. This church has been grounded in sound doctrine, but they need more understanding, particularly on (1) the supremacy of Christ, (2) the true image of God, (3) Christ's sacrificial death, and (4) the power of his resurrection. Paul's understanding of Jesus is contained in the Christian hymn quoted in Colossians 1:15–18a. This hymn was probably already in use in the early church. Its tribute to the supremacy of Christ comes from the creation account in Genesis, and it shows thoughtful reflection on Jesus in the Old Testament.

Paul then turns to Christ's work of redemption on the cross. Christians, once "alienated from God," are now reconciled to God and made "holy in his sight, without blemish" (Col. 1:21–23). The church is the community of saints in whom Christ dwells. This "mystery" had not been made known "for ages" (1:26)—that is, it was not revealed to the earliest patriarchs in Old Testament times. Paul's own commission as an apostle to the Gentiles was, in part, intended to make this mystery known. He desires a firm foundation in the faith with no slippage into areas of false doctrine or practice.

The Colossians face dangers of "hollow and deceptive philosophy," which depend "on human tradition and the basic principles of this world rather than on Christ" (Col. 2:8). Paul contrasts these with the "fullness of the Deity" found in Christ (2:9). For Christians, knowing Christ is all-sufficient. In him is the power of God to save sinners and give them a new heart. Such power can never be found in human wisdom, no matter how subtle or high-minded it may be. The focus of our lives may never be an elaborate philosophy, a list of rules, or religious festivals; it is the simple message of the crucified Christ. The religious celebrations found throughout the Old Testament all point to the death of Christ and the new life found in him, but they are mere shadows and should never eclipse the central importance of Christ's death.

What does it mean to live a new life in Christ? It means looking forward with eager expectation to Christ's return, not living according to the standards and patterns of one's former life, practicing godly virtues in the church, in the home, and at work, and always being ready to proclaim the gospel to others. Paul closes with a lengthy series of greetings to people, including Mark (Col. 4:10) and Luke (4:14)—two individuals who, according to early tradition, wrote the second and third Gospels.

1 Thessalonians

This letter is written to a church that has suffered much. Like the Old Testament prophets, the believers in Thessalonica "suffered from their own countrymen" when they received the gospel. Paul knows they have weathered the persecution well, and he wants to encourage them further. He himself delivered the gospel to them under great persecution—afflictions that demonstrated his commitment to Christ and his love for them. The focus of the book is their eager expectation of the return of Jesus, the Son of God, "from heaven," who will rescue them "from the coming wrath" (1 Thess. 1:10).

In light of the Lord's return and the hope of his appearing, Paul stresses the importance of godly living. It is God's will that believers be holy and abstain from sexual immorality (1 Thess. 4:3–5). No one should wrong or take advantage of a fellow believer; rather, each one should practice brotherly love, attempting to live a quiet life by working with his or her own hands (4:6–11). Such a life will not only win the respect of those outside the church, but also enable one not to "be dependent on anybody" (4:12).

To encourage their continued faithfulness and patience, Paul summarizes the events that will surround Christ's return. Jesus, who himself died and rose again, will return with those who have died. He will come down out of heaven with a shout and sound of a trumpet, and the "dead in Christ" will rise from their graves to meet him. After that, those Christians still alive will be gathered up into the air to meet him (1 Thess. 4:13–18).

But what is the time of the Lord's return and the sequence of events? No one knows. His coming will take most by surprise, but his true followers will be ready, watching and waiting for his return (1 Thess. 5:1–11). Paul closes his letter with several instructions for maintaining unity in the church: respect your leaders, work hard, be patient, be kind to each other, always be joyful, pray continually, and give thanks in all circumstances. In light of the Lord's return, holy living and godliness is essential.

2 Thessalonians

The believers in Thessalonica have remained steadfast in their faith in spite of hardship and persecution, but they need encouragement, especially since rumors and reports are circulating that Jesus has already returned. Paul thus writes a letter to comfort these faithful Christians and to affirm that though Jesus has not yet appeared, their hope in his return is not misplaced. Jesus will return, establish his kingdom, and judge the world.

Paul begins with a glowing report of the faith and endurance of the Thessalonians in spite of "persecutions and trials" (2 Thess. 1:4). Their suffering shows that they are "worthy of the kingdom of God" for which they are suffering. God is just, and their sufferings will be redressed "when the Lord Jesus is revealed from heaven in blazing fire with his powerful angels" (1:5–7).

Because forged letters have been circulating among the churches that Jesus has already returned, Paul disclaims their authenticity. His argument, based on the proper sequence of events, is biblical. Already when he was with them in person, he recounted the events related to Lord's return (2 Thess. 2:5). He knows through Old Testament prophecies that the coming of the kingdom of God must be preceded by the appearance of "the man of lawlessness," an individual (or nation) who "will exalt himself over everything that is called God" (2:3–4).

In Daniel this person is called the "fourth kingdom, strong as iron—for iron breaks and smashes everything" (Dan. 2:40), the "fourth beast—terrifying and frightening and very powerful" (7:7), the little horn that came out of the fourth beast (7:8), "the ruler who will come" (9:26), or the king who "will exalt and magnify himself above every god and will say unheard-of things against the God of gods" (11:36). This ruler rebels against God and his people for a little while, but soon the Son of Man will come from heaven, destroy him, and establish an eternal kingdom (7:23–28). Paul's reference here to the person who sets himself up in the temple and proclaims himself to be God is a reference to Daniel 9:27: "And on a wing [of the temple] he will set up an abomination that causes desolation."

The apostle's point is clear. Though "the secret power of lawlessness is already at work," this individual has not yet been revealed. Therefore, the Lord cannot yet have returned. He is sure that the Thessalonian Christians will not be deceived by this Antichrist. God has chosen them, and they will stand firm in that day by holding on to the teachings they have received from him.

1 Timothy

Paul writes this letter as a manual for the young pastor Timothy. He stresses the importance of sound doctrine that leads to godly living and warns him of the inherent dangers of church life in a fallen world, especially false teachers and false doctrine. Thus the church and its leadership should prepare themselves well for the work of the ministry by choosing competent leaders and avoiding dishonest and unethical ones.

Paul's first instructions concern what Timothy should do and say to the false teachers. He must examine his teaching and that of others by the type of life that instruction produces. Correct teaching in the grace of God will result in godly living. False teachers, on the other hand, have "wandered away [from sincere faith] . . . and turned to meaningless talk" (1 Tim. 1:6); they have no understanding of the things they are teaching. Paul's own former wicked way of life was transformed "as an example for those who would believe on him and receive eternal life" (1:16).

Paul admonishes Timothy to ensure that the life of the church be maintained and sustained through prayer. The men of the church are to pray "without anger or disputing" (1 Tim. 2:8); the women are to attend the worship services dressed modestly and must clothe themselves with good deeds (2:10), "learning in quietness and full submission" (2:11). They must not "teach or . . . have authority over a man" but must "be silent" in the worship service (2:12). Paul bases this on Adam's being created first and then his wife, Eve; hence the Scriptures assign to the husband a primary responsibility for his family's well-being (2:13).

Paul lists, in summary fashion, the requirements of an "overseer" or elder in the church. He must be a sober-minded, amiable, family man, who knows Scripture and can apply it to the life of the church. Deacons have essentially the same requirements. Church leaders should expect that "some will abandon the faith and follow deceiving spirits" (1 Tim. 4:1). The task of Timothy and other pastors, who have been "brought up in the truths of the faith and of good teaching" (4:6), is to "point these things out to the brothers" (4:6).

Personally, Timothy must manifest an example of diligence and devotion in sound doctrine and godly living. The treatment of widows requires considerable attention (1 Tim. 5:3–16). Teaching elders must be given double honor (5:17–19), and servants are to give their masters respect and honor (6:1–2). Paul concludes his letter with a renewed warning against false teachers, who are seeking to make a profit from their teaching (6:3–10). Such men are "conceited and understand nothing" (6:4).

2 Timothy

Conditions in the churches were becoming more troublesome. Godly leaders such as Timothy were coming close to losing heart, while false teachers were becoming more and more impudent in their teaching and actions. Thus Paul begins with an impassioned appeal to Timothy to "fan into flame the gift of God" and not be timid, but to have a "spirit of power, of love and of self-discipline" (2 Tim. 1:6–7). Paul admonishes him boldly to testify about the Lord (1:7).

The gospel was planned and given by God "before the beginning of time" (2 Tim. 1:9) and has now been revealed through the appearing of Jesus. Such a gospel inevitably stirs up opposition and invites distortion. All the more important, then, is it to remain faithful to the teaching received from Paul. Throughout all Asia, says Paul, he himself has been deserted (1:15–18). But he remains faithful and so now pleads with Timothy to do the same (2:1–2). Like a good soldier, a successful athlete, or a hardworking farmer, Timothy must focus on the work of the Lord rather than on worldly affairs (2:3–7).

In times of trouble, it is important to concentrate on the essentials of the gospel. One must know precisely why and for what he is suffering. In this case it centers on the resurrection of Jesus and on his claim to be the Davidic Messiah (2 Tim. 2:8). Moreover, Paul's confidence in God's election enables him to "endure everything" (2:10). Timothy's task is to keep reminding those in the church of the teaching of God's Word. He should study it well, focus on the central points, and know how to answer serious questions that arise. Those who oppose his instruction "he must gently instruct," leaving the task of changing their minds to God (2:25).

Some groups, however, are impossible to teach. They are the godless, who will arise in increasing numbers as the Lord's return approaches. Their motives are impure, they are unteachable, and "their folly will be clear to everyone" (2 Tim. 3:9). Timothy should have nothing to do with them. But Paul's teaching has been thoroughly tested and proven. Thus Timothy should continue in those teachings, knowing that they are grounded in the Old Testament Scriptures, which are God-breathed (3:16); in them the salvation that comes through faith in Christ Jesus is taught (3:15b).

Therefore, Paul instructs Timothy, "preach the Word" at all times (2 Tim. 4:2), exercising great patience and careful instruction. He must continue in God's Word even if the time comes when those who hear his teaching will not be able to endure it. They will leave him and follow teachers who say what they want to hear. That, Paul suggests, has already begun to happen to him. In his final personal instructions, Paul appropriately asks for his "scrolls" and "parchments" (4:12)—that is, his copies of Scripture.

Titus

Writing to Titus in Crete, Paul gives instructions on carrying out church ministry, much like he had given Timothy. His central concern is combating false and devious teachers; Paul stresses that Christians will make a clear defense of the gospel only by living a life that is beyond reproach. If each member of the church pays close attention to self-control and godliness, the church will grow in sound doctrine, and the work of the Lord will prosper. Of central importance is the hope of eternal life, "which God, who does not lie, promised before the beginning of time" (Titus 1:2) and which was entrusted to Paul "by the command of God" (1:3). A Christian's entire life is be lived in light of this hope—the "blessed hope" of Christ's return that motivates believers to live a godly life (cf. 2:13).

There was work left on Crete for Titus to complete, among which was appointing elders in every town. Thus Paul reviews the qualifications Titus should look for (Titus 1:6–9). This is necessary because of numerous false teachers ruining the churches and seeking dishonest gain by their teaching. Such people must be dealt with decisively before they do any further damage. How? Paul's answer is simple: "You must teach what is in accord with sound doctrine." Older men are to be taught to act worthy of respect; older women are to live in reverence, not slandering others but teaching what is good; younger women are to "love their husbands and children" and provide a good home for them; younger men are to be self-controlled; household servants are to carry out their duties faithfully and honestly.

In every occupation and within every relationship, Christians must reject ungodliness and live "self-controlled, upright and godly lives" (Titus 2:12) as they await the return of Christ. They must live in subjection to the "rulers and authorities" (3:1) and always be ready to do what is good. Paul grounds this call to godliness in the nature of the gospel itself. In Christ, believers have been washed, saved, and renewed by the Holy Spirit in order "to devote themselves to doing what is good" (3:8).

Paul concludes with personal greetings and an explanation of the practical importance of sound doctrine: "Our people must learn to devote themselves to doing what is good, in order that they may provide for daily necessities and not live unproductive lives" (Titus 3:14).

Philemon

After a brief greeting, Paul begins his letter to Philemon (apparently a resident of Colosse; Col. 4:9) by acknowledging the work of God in Philemon's life and ministry and his "love for all the saints" (Philem. 5). The main point in the letter is an appeal to Philemon on behalf of Onesimus, a former household servant of his (v. 16) who had apparently escaped to Rome, subsequently met Paul, and accepted the gospel. Thus both Philemon and Onesimus are in Paul's eternal debt.

Paul urges Philemon pastorally to accept Onesimus back as a brother in Christ (Philem. 16). This may mean accepting him back as a servant and, as such, treating him in a Christian manner, or it may mean releasing him from servant status. In either case it will be a great display of the power of the gospel within the context of the ancient world. Paul, with apostolic authority, could order Philemon to accept Onesimus, but that will hardly have the effect of a voluntary act of brotherly love. Paul wants Philemon's actions to be "spontaneous and not forced" (v. 14). He is fully confident that Philemon will accept Onesimus with open arms (v. 21); nevertheless, he offers to pay any outstanding debts or penalties Onesimus may owe (v. 17).

This short book clearly owes its acceptance within the New Testament canon to the fact that it speaks directly to an issue that lies not far beneath the surface of the Bible—the effect of the gospel on the existing social structures of the ancient world. The Bible clearly opposes involuntary slavery. In 1 Timothy 1:10, for example, Paul reckons "slave traders" along with "the ungodly and sinful, the unholy and irreligious." But what is the impact of the gospel on those economic structures that include servants, who are bound to their masters under the full force of the law? In 1 Timothy 6:1–2, Paul stated that servants should treat their masters with respect, even when they are believing masters. But what about believing masters' treatment of believing servants? This book becomes the occasion for Paul to urge that just as Christians servants must respect their Christian masters, so Christian masters are to accept and respect their Christian servants as brothers in Christ, even when they have wronged them.

Hebrews

The central theme of this book is the work of Jesus Christ as the mediator of the new covenant. Jesus is the eternal Son of God, the only mediator between God and humans. He is far superior to the angels, even though God made him lower than the angels "for a little while" (see NIV note on Heb. 2:7). Unlike the high priesthood of the house of Aaron, Jesus, by his incarnation and resurrection, became a high priest "of the same family" (2:11) as all humanity. His mediatorial priesthood can thus claim superiority to that of Aaron.

Melchizedek was both a king and a priest (Gen. 14:18); hence he was a particularly apt image of Christ's priesthood. The messianic priesthood, exemplified in Melchizedek, was superior to the priesthood of the house of Aaron. The latter priesthood was always temporary and, as such, had to be superseded. In the office of priest occupied by Jesus, there is both an eternal priesthood and an eternal priest. Christ, the Son of God, did not offer a sacrifice in a sanctuary made "by man" but in "the true tabernacle set up by the Lord" in heaven (Heb. 8:1–2).

The details of Israel's worship at the tabernacle contain many spiritual lessons, the center of which was the annual Day of Atonement. God showed the inadequacy of this blood sacrifice offered by the high priest by commanding that it be repeated yearly and be offered not only for the people but also for the high priest. In a *once-for-all* act as high priest of the new covenant, Christ offered *his own* blood as sacrifice in the heavenly tabernacle. He has thus become the mediator of the new covenant, offering eternal salvation through his death.

The readers of this letter have fared well in their faith in past times, but they face a uncertain future. Therefore, the writer calls them to continue in well-doing—exercising brotherly love and hospitality, visiting the mistreated, being faithful in marriage, showing contentment, trusting in God, bearing disgrace for Christ's sake, offering praise, sharing with others, and submitting to authority (Heb. 13). They must not "shrink back" from receiving the promises. The author holds out to them both the hope of the imminent return of Christ (10:35–39) and the commendable examples of faithfulness in the past (11:1–40). He repeatedly demonstrates the importance of looking to the Old Testament Scriptures not only for instruction in God's plan of salvation but also as a source of comfort in the life of the Christian.

James

The book of James begins with an exposition of divine wisdom regarding two specific areas of a Christian's life: trials (James 1:2–18) and obedience to Scripture (1:19–27). Curiously, this is precisely where the book of Hebrews concludes, exhorting believers to persevere in trials (cf. Heb. 12:1). The lesson is the same: God uses testing and trials as a way of perfecting faith (James 1:4; cf. Heb. 12:5–6). In the midst of trials one should ask: What is the "wisdom" God intends to teach by means of this trial? Unlike worldly wisdom, divine wisdom does not come from mere observation. It comes from prayer and divine illumination (James 1:5), unwavering faith (1:6–8), and reflective listening to God's Word, implanted in a godly life (1:19–21).

James gives three examples of the application of the divine wisdom he describes in the first chapter. (1) Humility (James 2:1–13). Giving preferential treatment to the wealthy and mistreating the poor violate the central message of the law to "love your neighbor as yourself" (2:8). (2) Faith and works (2:14–26). The faith by which one is saved (2:14) must be a living faith that produces action (2:17). Thus, works of love serve as evidence of saving faith—for example, Abraham's offering of Isaac (see Gen. 22). (3) The tongue (James 3:1–12). Teachers must talk. Thus they risk a stricter judgment and should be doubly careful of what they say (cf. 2:12), knowing, however, that they are not perfect and "stumble in many ways" (3:2). The real problem of the tongue lies in lack of control (3:3–8), for it can be an instrument of both praise and cursing (3:9–12).

The test of divine wisdom lies in its results. Earthly wisdom stems from envy and selfish ambition and produces disorder (James 3:14–16); divine wisdom stems from a pure heart and produces peace and righteousness (3:17–18). Behind the instruction of biblical wisdom lies the overwhelming confidence in divine justice. God alone metes out reward and retribution for human action. All that the believer can do is rest in the all-encompassing will of God (4:11–16) and do what he or she knows to be good (4:17).

Where does the hope of the Christian life fit? For James it lies in the future fulfillment of God's eternal plan: "Be patient, then, brothers, until the Lord's coming" (James 5:7). The rich and the proud, though they prosper now, are only storing up divine judgment for themselves when Christ returns (5:1–6). The book of Job is a paradigm of God's ultimate vindication of the righteous wise man (5:11). The wise person is one who trusts God in all things and waits for him to fulfill his promises. But there is still much room for prayer (5:13–15) and confession of sin (5:16). Elijah is an example of the effective prayer of a righteous person (5:16–18).

1 Peter

God's elect, as "strangers in the world" (1 Peter 1:1), eagerly await the return of the Lord to establish his kingdom. In this world we suffer painful trials, which test our faith. But we have a better hope when Christ's "glory is revealed" in his second coming. The resurrection of Christ is the starting point of this hope. The Old Testament prophets themselves searched intently in their writings to know the time and circumstances of Christ's coming, though they were well aware that what they wrote about would not happen in their own day but in the future (1:10–12).

Christians must always live in light of the hope of Christ's soon return (1 Peter 1:13). They must not act according to the standards of this world but as strangers whose values are measured in terms of silver and gold (1:17–18); they are at home in the presence of a holy God who has purchased them "with the precious blood of Christ" (1:19).

The church is composed of those born of the enduring Word of God (1 Peter 1:23). Believers form a "spiritual house to be a holy priesthood" (2:5). God's Word is written on their hearts (Jer. 31:33) by God's Spirit (Ezek. 36:26). They are "living stones," offering "spiritual sacrifices" (1 Peter 2:5); they are a "chosen people, a royal priesthood, a holy nation" (2:9).

Christians must "live such good lives among the pagans" so that many will turn to Jesus Christ in faith and thus "glorify God on the day he visits us" (that is, at Christ's second coming; 1 Peter 2:12). They must abstain from worldly desires (2:11–12), submit to authority (2:13–17), and live in harmony with each other (3:8–12). Servants must submit to their master (2:18–25), wives must submit to husbands (3:1–6), and husbands must respect wives (3:7). In this way, they will call attention to themselves in a wicked world. They should always be ready "to give an answer to everyone who asks" the reason for their hope (3:13–15) and be ready to suffer for doing good (3:16–17). Through the resurrection, Christians become members of Christ's kingdom, over which he reigns at God's right hand (3:22). As members of that kingdom they must live according to God's will and not in the ways of their former lives (4:1–6). Their one hope should be fixed on the return of Christ (4:7–11). Christians themselves should rejoice that they "participate in the sufferings of Christ" (4:12–19).

Elders must oversee the church not by lording over them or acting greedily but by being "examples to the flock" (1 Peter 5:3–4). Young men should submit to the elders. Everyone is to be humble and self-controlled (5:6–9), trusting God for strength and power (5:10–11).

2 Peter

By this letter Peter hopes to strengthen his readers' knowledge of God and Jesus through an emphasis on sound doctrine. He begins by discussing the importance of a well-balanced knowledge. For Peter, knowledge of Jesus is an important link in a believer's possession of divine power (2 Peter 1:3). The starting point is faith (1:5) and the goal is love (1:7), but to both of these must be added goodness, knowledge, self-control, perseverance, godliness, and brotherly kindness (1:5–8). Such qualities of life will keep a Christian "from being ineffective and unproductive in [his] knowledge" of the Lord Jesus Christ (1:8).

Christians need to be continually reminded of Christ's power in their lives (2 Peter 1:12–15). Peter, who at this time is about to give his own life as a martyr for the Lord (cf. John 21:18–19), reminds his readers that he was a eyewitness to the honor and glory Christ received from the Father at his transfiguration (cf. Matt. 17:5; Mark 9:7; Luke 9:35): "We ourselves heard this voice that came from heaven when we were with him on the sacred mountain" (2 Peter 1:18). Not only can he claim his own eyewitness account of Christ's glory, but there is also "the word of the [Old Testament] prophets" that has proved even more certain (1:19). That prophetic word is like "a light shining in a dark place" (1:19b; cf. Ps. 119:105); reading and meditating on Scripture dispels the darkness of the mind. The prophets themselves did not devise these prophecies about Jesus; rather, they were "carried along by the Holy Spirit" (2 Peter 1:20–21).

Peter then warns about false teachers in the church, who, motivated by greed, bring swift destruction by their teaching (2 Peter 2:1–4). Peter assures his readers that, though it may delay, God's judgment always falls on these ungodly people. Thus true believers must have nothing to do with them, for they have turned away from Christ. Because they pervert God's Word, they are worse off than when they had no knowledge of the gospel (2:17–22).

Peter feels he must explain God's delay in Christ's second coming. Some were saying that God would not intervene in judgment in human affairs and creation because he had never done so in the past (2 Peter 3:3–4). The truth of the matter is that God did intervene in human affairs by bringing judgment in the days of the Flood (3:5–6). In delaying his coming, God is not slow about keeping his promise. He is patient, wanting to give everyone—even the ungodly—time to repent and turn to him. But the time of the end will ultimately come; when it does, the ungodly and all the evil in God's creation will be destroyed by fire (3:10–12).

1 John

The author of this letter is an eyewitness of "the Word of life" (1 John 1:1–2), which he saw and touched (that is, Jesus; cf. John 1:1–14) and to which he now testifies. Jesus, God's Son, is the "atoning sacrifice" for sin (1 John 2:2). Through his blood those who walk in God's light are purified from all sin (1:7). Those who do not walk in God's light are liars, even though they claim to have fellowship with him (1:6). Walking in fellowship entails a continuous confession of sin and dependence on Jesus' atoning death.

Christians must maintain an upright relationship with God through confession and repentance. Walking as Jesus walked is not "a new command but an old one" (1 John 2:7), which they "have had since the beginning"—that is, the command to love one another (Lev. 19:18; Deut. 30:6b). Anyone who lives in the light will love his or her fellow believer (2:9–11).

Some in the church have fallen away; this proves they never truly belonged to Christ (1 John 2:19). Those who have a genuine "anointing from the Holy One" will never fall away, though they still need to be warned (2:20–26). The only safeguard against falling away is to hold firmly to the teachings of Jesus (2:27).

The central question about Jesus is whether he is the Christ, that is, the Messiah (1 John 2:22). Is he the heavenly Son of Man who, in his death and resurrection, has received the kingdom and the people promised him before the foundation of the earth (cf. Dan. 7:9–14; John 17:1–5)? To deny that Jesus is the Christ is to deny "the Father and the Son" (1 John 2:22); to accept Jesus as the Christ is to accept the Trinitarian confession of Jesus as Lord.

The distinguishing characteristics of the true children of God are righteousness (1 John 2:29–3:10), love (3:11–20), and faith (3:21–24). Christians must test the spirits of those who claim to speak in God's name (4:1–6). Do they acknowledge that "Jesus Christ has come in the flesh"? Every spirit that "does not [thus] acknowledge Jesus" is not from God but is "the spirit of the antichrist" (4:2–3). John moves beyond this confessional test to give a more general criterion for distinguishing the true from the false: True believers listen to God's Word and to those who proclaim it (4:6). To this he adds the test of love (4:7–5:4): "Whoever does not love does not know God, because God is love" (4:7–8).

Jesus, the Son of God, "is the one who came by water and blood" (1 John 5:6); that is, he came in the flesh (cf. 4:2). The Spirit bears witness to him (5:6b) by means of an internal testimony: "Anyone who believes in the Son of God has this testimony in his heart" (5:10). What testimony? It is the eternal life given in the Son (5:11–12).

2 John

The author of this letter is identified only as "the elder" (2 John 1). The close association of this book with 1 John and the Fourth Gospel has led to the identification of its author as John, though strictly speaking he is anonymous. This letter summarizes 1 John, focusing on the main points of that letter (walking in Christ, brotherly love, and false doctrine) and adding a warning against inadvertently sharing in the work of the antichrists (vv. 10–11). Note that 3 John takes these same themes and applies them to a specific church situation.

The book is addressed to "the chosen lady and her children" (2 John 1). This is usually taken to mean a local church, though some refer it to a specific house church in the home of a prominent woman. That the letter closes with a greeting from "the children of your chosen sister" suggests that these are titles given to various church bodies and not specific individuals.

John begins by focusing on the central themes of 1 John—the Trinitarian notion of Jesus Christ as God's Son and the theme of truth and love (2 John 3). As in 1 John 1:5–2:2, he emphasizes the importance of maintaining a consistent walk with Christ (2 John 4). The importance of this walk includes the command to love one another (2 John 5; cf. 1 John 2:7). Walking in the light also means walking in love (2 John 6; cf. 1 John 5:3).

Love involves trust, and thus John warns his readers to "watch out" for the "many deceivers, who do not acknowledge Jesus Christ as coming in the flesh" (2 John 7; cf. 1 John 4:2–3) and who cause them to lose their reward (2 John 8). The test of true discipleship is continuing "in the teaching of Christ," that is, the teaching about Jesus as the Son of God who has come in bodily form to give himself as an "atoning sacrifice for our sins" (1 John 2:2). John heightens his warning regarding these false teachers by urging his readers to give no support whatever to them. Even to welcome such teachers is to participate in their work (2 John 11). The close of the letter anticipates 3 John, for the author still has "much to write," though his immediate intention is to visit them "and talk . . . face to face" (2 John 12).

3 John

This letter is a virtual replay of 2 John, with one difference: where 2 John deals with general principles, 3 John gives concrete examples in the life of a specific church. Like 2 John, the three primary themes are walking in Christ, brotherly love, and false doctrine. The author addresses a specific individual, Gaius, who was a leader in a local church. The introduction establishes that the writer and Gaius fundamentally agree in the teachings of Christ.

In both 1 John 1:5–2:2 and 2 John 4, the writer begins by emphasizing the importance of a consistent walk with Christ. Here he commends Gaius for continuing "to walk in the truth" (3 John 3). In other words, Gaius is a concrete example of John's teaching in the other letters. Furthermore, Gaius is an example of walking in brother love (v. 6; cf. 1 John 2:7; 2 John 5).

In his earlier letters, John repeatedly warned his readers of false teachers, giving two kinds of tests. (1) The doctrinal test: Do they acknowledge Jesus as coming in the flesh (1 John 4:2–3; 2 John 7)? (2) The practical test: Do they exercise love (1 John 4:7–12)? Gaius is now presented with two opposing examples of professing teachers in the church, Diotrephes and Demetrius. He must apply John's tests to distinguish between the two.

John describes Diotrephes as one "who loves to be first" and "will have nothing to do with us" (3 John 9). He is "gossiping maliciously" and "refuses to welcome the brothers" (v. 10). Demetrius, on the other hand, "is well spoken of by everyone—and even by the truth itself" (v. 12). That is, his life is consistent with the teaching of Christ. The choice between these two teachers, then, is clear: "Anyone who does what is good is from God" (v. 11).

Within the present canonical order of the New Testament books, the writer's concluding statement that he still has "much to write" (3 John 13; cf. 2 John 12) anticipates the book of Revelation, John's final work. It may also be a veiled apology for the brevity of the letter. It is clear from the letter itself, however, that the writer only intends this to refer to his desire to talk to his readers "face to face" rather than write any more (3 John 14).

Jude

The book of Jude warns readers against the clever devices of the false teachers among them. Their false teaching may be new, but their error, manifested as an ungodly manner of life, is as old as time. For him, the question boils down to the authority by which these men teach. They claim their own authority, whereas Jude warns his readers to remain faithful to the doctrine they have already been taught.

Jude moves quickly into a scathing denunciation of the heretics (Jude 4). What is at stake is nothing less than a perversion of God's grace into "license for immorality" (v. 4b) and a denial of Jesus (v. 4c). Their threat is the same as the apostasy of Israel in the desert: Those whom God delivered from Egypt, he later destroyed because they did not believe (v. 5; cf. Num. 14:11; 20:12). Even the angels, who were created to be with God, "did not keep their positions of authority" and were subsequently "bound with everlasting chains for judgment" (Jude 6). Jude probably has in mind the fall of Satan and his angels alluded to in Ezekiel 28:11–19.

Jude warns the churches that the false teachers "pollute their own bodies, reject authority and slander celestial beings," the same way that people at Sodom acted (Jude 8; cf. Gen. 19:5–9). They reject all authority but their own; thus these men assume more authority than even Michael, the archangel. According to a popular story about the death of Moses, known to Jude and his readers but no longer available to us, Michael refused to condemn even Satan, being content to call on God to rebuke him (Jude 9). Such respect for divine authority cannot be found among these false teachers (v. 10). They are like Cain, who refused to pay heed to God's warning (Gen. 4:6–12), and like Balaam and Korah, who sought to profit from the work of God (vv. 11, 17). Jude reassures his readers that divine judgment is awaiting these ungodly men (vv. 14–16).

Jude's final appeal is to the authority of Jesus and the apostles—in this case, Peter's reference to the words of Scripture in 2 Peter 3:2–3, "In the last times there will be scoffers who will follow their own ungodly desires" (Jude 18–19). Jude then elaborates, describing false teachers as those who divide the people, who follow their own "natural instincts," and who do not have the Spirit (v. 19). In opposition to such men, Jude's readers should build themselves up by paying attention to doctrine ("faith"), prayer, love, and mercy (vv. 20–23).

Jude closes the letter with a formal doxology that stresses God's power to preserve believers until the time of Christ's return.

Revelation

The last book of the New Testament describes itself as a "revelation" of final cataclysmic events about to transpire on the earth. Its central character is Jesus, "the faithful witness, the firstborn from the dead, and the ruler of the kings of the earth" (Rev. 1:5). These titles stress his death, resurrection, and exaltation over believers and his ultimate victory over the nations.

In his first vision, John sees Jesus as One like the Son of Man, coming to judge the saints (Rev. 1:9–3:22; cf. Dan. 7:9–10). As in Daniel, first comes divine judgment, then the Son of Man establishes his kingdom. The churches addressed by Christ (Rev. 2–3) represent all churches at that time.

Revelation 4–19 contains a rich assortment of events. John sees a vision of the throne room of heaven and a scroll with seven seals, each of which is opened by the Lamb of God (chs. 4–7) and brings with it a cataclysmic event. Then comes the blasts of seven trumpets (chs. 8–11), which in turn is followed by a battle scene with great beasts and wicked powers (chs. 12–14). Then comes a vision of seven plagues (chs. 15–16), concluding with a vision of the fall of Babylon (chs. 17–19).

Does John write these events in the order that they are to occur? Or are they simply listed without regard to sequence? Since these events are portrayed in symbolic language, their meaning is not self-evident. Moreover, they owe their interpretation to other portions of Scripture, such as Daniel 7; Ezekiel 38–39; and Matthew 24. To gain an understanding of the book, one should first survey the events of the book in their symbolic dress, without interpretation. After a sense of the order of the book has been obtained, one can develop the order and the meaning of the figurative events.

The fall of Babylon at the conclusion of the book is accompanied by a battle of the armies of heaven, led by someone mounted on a white horse whose name is "the Word of God" (Rev. 19:11-16). This is a picture of Christ (cf. 20:4), "KING OF KINGS AND LORD OF LORDS" (19:16). At his appearance he defeats the Antichrist, the false prophet, and the wicked kings (19:17–21). The dragon (Satan) is bound in chains and cast into the Abyss for one thousand years (20:1–3). At the end of those years, the dragon is released, gathers together all the nations (Gog and Magog), and attacks Jerusalem. He is defeated by fire from heaven and cast into a burning lake.

The last act of judgment is a great court session in which all of the dead are gathered and the deeds of each are read off from the books kept in the court (cf. Dan. 7:10). In the midst of this vision John sees the new Jerusalem, in which God will again dwell with humankind, just as in the garden of Eden in the beginning (Gen. 2). The city is described in detail (Rev. 21:9–27). As in the garden of Eden, a river flows through it and waters "the tree of life" (22:1–2). In this city the curse of Genesis 3 has been removed (Rev. 22:3). God, once again, lives with his people in an eternal kingdom (22:4–5).

Glossary

Abrahamic Covenant

Genesis 12:1–3; 15:9–21; 17:1–14

God promised Abraham that his descendants become a great nation and enjoy his blessing; through them the rest of humanity would be blessed. This Abrahamic covenant is the basis of God's dealings with Israel and the rest of humanity in the rest of the Bible. All God's present and future promises are fulfillments of God's promise to Abraham. Through the descendants of Abraham the Messiah came. The biblical basis of modern missions and evangelism is God's promise to bless "all the peoples on earth" (Gen. 12:3) through the descendants of Abraham, that is, through the Messiah, Jesus Christ. *See also* Blessing, Covenant

Atoning Sacrifice

See Sacrifices and Offerings (Atonement)

Babylonian Captivity

See Exile

Blessing

The concept of blessing is the Bible's way of expressing God's purpose and design for the creation of humanity. When God created the man and the woman, he blessed them, saying, "Be fruitful and increase in number; fill the earth and subdue it" (Gen. 1:28). This clearly entails the enjoyment of a full and enriched life of fellowship with God and one's own family. The Bible says elsewhere that children are a great reward from God: "Blessed is the man whose quiver is full of them" (Ps. 127:5). A key element in the biblical concept of blessing, according to the early chapters of Genesis, is the gift of eternal life. This was offered to all humanity in the Tree of Life (Gen. 2), but when the man and the woman forsook God's blessing and sought one of their own, they lost access to it (Gen. 3). The rest of the Bible is a story of God's gracious offer of the blessing of eternal life. The preeminent blessing that the Messiah brings to all humanity is "life forevermore" (Ps. 133:3) or "eternal life" (John 3:16).

The Canon of Scripture

See Introduction

Covenant

Strictly speaking, a covenant is a legal contract in which one or more parties bind themselves to certain agreements. Promises are made and faithfulness to the covenant is measured by the fulfillment of those promises. God made various covenants with humankind and his world. In Genesis, for example, God made a covenant with Noah and all living creatures that he would never again destroy the world with a flood (Gen. 9:8–11). This is called the Noahic Covenant. *See also* Abrahamic Covenant, Mosaic Covenant, Davidic Covenant, and New Covenant

Davidic Covenant

2 Samuel 7

When God chose David as king over Israel, he entered a covenant with him regarding the future of both his dynasty and kingdom. God promised that a son would be born to his house who would build a temple in Jerusalem and rule gloriously over the people of God. Initially, the fulfillment of that covenant appeared to lie in the reign of Solomon, the son of David, who built the first temple in Jerusalem. Solomon, however, proved unworthy of that honor, and the promise was passed on to the subsequent generations of Davidic kings, none of whom proved worthy of the promise. The hope for the fulfillment of the Davidic covenant was thus transferred to the future; or, to say it another way, from the beginning of the Old Testament Scriptures, the focus of God's promise to David was always on the future "seed" or descendant of David, who was the Messiah. Thus the Davidic covenant lies at the heart of the messianic prophecies of the Old Testament; those prophecies are fulfilled in the life and death of Jesus, the Son of David.

Eschatology

Throughout the Bible is a persistent hope that in the future God will intervene in the affairs of this world and do a mighty work by restoring creation and accomplishing redemption. This study is called *eschatology* (taken from the Greek word for the "last things," *eschaton*). God created all things good. But humanity rebelled; hence all of God's good creation was subjected to the curse. God's act of redemption in sending his Son to die on the cross removed the penalty of sin and provided for a new humanity and a new creation. The completion of those two new things lies in the future, when God will break into the present order of creation and renew all things. He began that work with the coming of Christ, but will finish it only when Christ returns to establish his kingdom. Thus, *eschatology* can refer to the first coming of Christ or to his second coming to establish his kingdom. The Old Testament does not divide the Messiah's coming into a first coming and a second coming; that became necessary only after the Messiah was rejected and the consummation of his kingdom was delayed. Thus an eschatological text in the Old Testament may find its fulfill-ment in the first coming or second coming of Christ. *See* Messianic

The Exile (or Babylonian Captivity)

The exile was a historical event in the life of the people of Israel, in which their country and cities were destroyed and they were taken captive into Babylon (this happened in the sixth century B.C.). This was more than a mere historical event, however, for it also meant that God, who had endured cen-turies of rebellion on the part of his chosen people, was finally bringing about the due penalty for Israel's sin. God is a just God—a God of mercy and a God of wrath. His mercy was shown in his long delay of sending Israel into cap-tivity; his justice in the destruction of the nation by the Babylonians. The exile was of central importance to the biblical writers, for the Lord himself had become Israel's enemy. The people, who had for many centuries assumed that God would never destroy his own people, now faced the horrible reality that they were living in a foreign land and were captive to a foreign people. More-over, their own land lay in ruins. *See also* The Return from Captivity

Kingdom (Kingdom of God)

God is the King of all creation, and all creation is subject to him and his will. He cares for his world as a king cares for his subjects and realm. His law, the expression of his will, reigns throughout his realm. In the books of the Old Testament, God's kingdom is represented in his rule over the people of Israel. Israel was a theocracy (meaning "rule by God"; cf. Judg. 8:23). In the establishment of the Davidic kingship (*see* Davidic Covenant), the king-dom of Israel became the physical representation of the kingdom of God on earth, and God ruled through the house of David. The promised Son of David, the Messiah, was to rule over all the world from the throne of David (Ps. 2:8). In the Gospels, Jesus preached that the kingdom of God was on the verge of being established. Though he was rejected by his own countrymen and cru-cified by Rome, the New Testament writers do not give up hope that his king-dom will endure. The central message of the gospel is that those who put their faith in Christ become members of his kingdom and that the whole of his king-dom will be established at his future return.

Messiah, Messianic

Throughout the Bible is a recurring theme of fall and redemption (*see* Eschatology). God created the world good. But his world and its creatures rebelled and now stand in opposition to him. In God's grace, he promised to send a Redeemer—an individual who would defeat the forces of evil and establish a righteous kingdom (*see* Kingdom). This Redeemer, who would rule God's creation and all humanity, is variously described in the Bible. In the

Old Testament he is identified as a king from the tribe of Judah or the house of David. He is a prophet like Moses, a priest like Melchizedek, or the "Son of Man" who will return in the clouds of the heavens to establish his universal kingdom. In the New Testament the Redeemer is Jesus.

In the Old Testament the title *Messiah* is rarely, if ever, used of this coming Redeemer—the reason being that the word *messiah* (meaning "the anointed one") is used in a number of different ways. For example, it was a common title for the political king. In the New Testament, Jesus is primarily known as the Messiah, though in its Greek form, *Christos* ("the Christ"). Because of this lack of uniform terminology in the Bible, it is best to use the term "messianic" rather than "Messiah." The term *messianic* is used to describe any and all biblical passages that speak of a future redemption in light of an individual Redeemer.

Mosaic Covenant

Exodus 19–24

On several occasions throughout Israel's early history, God established, and renewed, a covenant between himself and his people. The central passages recounting that covenant are Exodus 19 and 24. In that covenant God promised Israel that they would be a great and wise nation if they would obey him and keep his commandments. Though Israel often transgressed the Mosaic covenant, as in the case of the Golden Calf (Ex. 32), God forgave them and continued his covenant relationship with them. Eventually Israel's rebellion caught up with them, however. The Mosaic covenant had stipulated (Deut. 4:26–27; 28:15–68) that if Israel failed to obey God's law, they would be carried away in exile from the Promised Land. That happened in the Babylonian captivity (*see* The Exile).

New Covenant

Jeremiah 31:31–34

As Israel's relationship with God under the Mosaic covenant progressed from bad to worse, God raised up prophets to proclaim that divine judgment for Israel lay just ahead if the people did not repent. Their failure to heed the prophets only served to seal the threat of judgment. God delivered his people over to their enemies, and they were taken into captivity (*see* Mosaic Covenant). But these same prophets who brought God's message of doom and destruction were also the heralds of another, more hopeful message—that this was not the end of their relationship with God, for God promised a new covenant. This covenant would not be like the Mosaic covenant, which presented Israel with a written law, with detailed stipulations that had to be kept. In the new covenant God's people would be changed. God would send his Spirit (Ezek. 36:24–28) and renew their hearts and minds (John 3:5–8). They would all obey God's will because it would be written on their hearts.

Central to the concept of the new covenant was the necessity of humanity's sin and guilt being atoned for once and for all. There was the need for a perfect redemption. This was accomplished by the death of Christ on the cross. Hence, on the eve of his death Jesus spoke of his crucifixion and his blood as the means of establishing the new covenant (Luke 22:20). *See* Sacrifices and Offerings (Atonement), Covenant

Noahic Covenant

See Covenant

Pentateuch

See The Torah

Remnant

A remnant is a small select group, distinguished from a larger group by their faithfulness and sincerity. That concept is already present in the Flood narratives of Genesis, for Noah and his family formed a faithful remnant amid a generation that had turned its back on God. When God later chose Abraham, he intended to form a nation, which would be a remnant of sorts among all the families of the earth. This nation was to be a kingdom of priests and a holy nation (Ex. 19:6). But it soon became evident that not all of the descendants of Abraham would prove faithful and follow God's call to live a holy life. Thus early in the biblical texts the concept of a faithful remnant within the larger group of God's people developed. As the people of God drifted further from his way, the focus of God's promises began to shift onto the shoulders of this faithful remnant. In the later prophetic books of the Old Testament, the hope for the future focused almost entirely on the remnant. Through the concept of the remnant, the promises to the fathers could find fulfillment even though the nation as a whole might suffer divine wrath.

The Return from Captivity

The Babylonian captivity was a central event in the life of God's people (*see* The Exile). It meant that God's people were themselves experiencing God's wrath. But the biblical writers also stressed that God's wrath against his own people would not last forever. God, who had allowed his people to be taken to Babylon, would also bring them out of captivity and back into the Promised Land. This return was a central focus of the hope that the prophets put before the people. The prophet Jeremiah, for example, foresaw that the Babylonian exile would last only seventy years, after which God's people would return to the land; this happened when King Cyrus of Persia issued an edict that allowed all who desired to return to the Promised Land. Though there was great hope that the return from Babylon might mean the fulfillment of the messianic hopes of the people, that did not happen. The coming of the Messiah was projected into a much more distant future (see Dan. 9:24–27).

Sacrifices and Offerings (Atonement)

Central to the rituals and holy actions described in the Bible is the concept of atonement. A holy and righteous God cannot overlook wickedness or lawlessness. Numerous examples in the Bible demonstrate that the only just penalty for blatant disobedience to God's will is death (e.g., Gen. 2:17). Human beings have strayed from God's way and sought their own means of finding blessing (*see* Blessing). But God is a gracious God (Ex. 34:6). In spite of Israel's repeated failures, he provided a means of substitution whereby the death rightly due sinful human beings was transferred to an innocent animal. The blood shed by that animal was accepted by God as a substitute for the blood of the guilty sinner. That system of sacrifice was God's gracious gift to atone for sin. The word *atonement* means, literally, "to be *at one* [atone] with."

There was, however, a latent inequity in its system of sacrifices. Already in the Old Testament that inequity is felt. David, for example, says in Psalm 51:15–16: "O Lord . . . you do not delight in sacrifice, or I would bring it; you do not take pleasure in burnt offerings." This same theme is picked up in the New Testament: "It is impossible for the blood of bulls and goats to take away sins" (Heb. 10:4). These sacrifices thus served more as a reminder of sin and the need for atonement than as the actual removal of guilt. They had to be repeated regularly in order to cover the guilt of the people. In other words, something more was necessary. That something, as the New Testament teaches, is "the sacrifice of the body of Jesus Christ once for all" (Heb. 10:10).

Sinai Covenant

See Mosaic Covenant

Tabernacle

The word tabernacle means simply "tent." The tabernacle was the tent in which God lived among his people. God is a holy God. Were he to live freely among his people, they would face the serious consequences of having a holy and righteous God in their midst. To safeguard the people and yet to ensure his own presence with them, God gave instructions to his people in the desert to build a dwelling for him. The primary purpose of the tabernacle was thus to provide adequate separation between God and the people. It was not to keep God from them, but keep them from improperly entering into his presence. The only proper entry of a sinful people into the presence of a holy God was through the blood of the sacrifice (*see* Sacrifices and Offerings [Atonement]). The construction of the tabernacle served as a basis for such sacrifices.

An important feature of the tabernacle was its portability. It was constructed so that it could be dismantled and carried along with the people. In that way God continued to live with Israel everywhere they were in the desert. They did not have to return regularly to Mount Sinai to meet with him. After they settled in the Promised Land, Israel built the temple, whose purpose was also to serve as a dwelling place for God. There he could be with his people, and they could come before him with sacrifices and offerings (cf. 1 Kings 8).

In the New Testament, the incarnation of Jesus is understood along lines similar to the tabernacle (John 1:14). When God took on a human nature, it was the ultimate act of condescension. God was no longer approached through the rituals of the tabernacle or temple; he was now living among us in bodily form.

The Torah (Pentateuch)

The Torah, the first section of the Old Testament, is made up of five parts. These parts—Genesis, Exodus, Leviticus, Numbers, and Deuteronomy—are usually considered individual books in their own right. In reality, they are merely five segments of the larger work called the *Pentateuch* (a Greek word meaning "five-part book"). The Hebrew word *Torah* means "instruction." The Torah is the foundational document of both the Old and the New Testaments. In it the central themes of the Bible are laid down and given their initial development. The subsequent books of the Bible develop these themes in a variety of ways.